Growing up in THE 1950s

C.A.R. Hills

Batsford Academic and Educational Limited London

© C. A. R. Hills 1983
First published 1983

Typeset by Tek-Art Ltd, London
and printed in Great Britain by
R. J. Acford Ltd.
Chichester, Sussex
for the publishers
Batsford Academic and Educational Ltd
an imprint of B. T. Batsford Ltd,
4 Fitzhardinge Street
London W1H 0AH

ISBN 0 7134 1367 0

Frontispiece: **Secondary schoolboys, 1956.**

Picture Acknowledgments

The Author and Publishers thank the following for
their kind permission to reproduce copyright
illustrations: Catherine Alderson, fig 2; BBC Hulton
Picture Library, figs 1, 5, 6, 10, 11, 12, 13, 18, 22,
23, 26, 27, 30, 32, 34, 35, 36, 39, 44, 46, 50, 54,
55, 56, 58, 59, 61, 63; BBC Photographs, figs 51, 52;
The Design Council, figs 20, 21; Alan Finlay, fig 33;
The Gas Council, fig 42; Henry Grant, frontispiece,
figs 7, 19, 24, 28, 38, 48, 60; Pat Hodgson Library,
fig 45; The Kobal Collection, fig 57; London Transport Executive, fig 40; Michael Ryan Photography,
fig 47; J. Sainsbury Ltd, fig 43; The Spectator, fig
64; G.H. Taylor, figs 14, 16; John Topham Picture
Library, figs 8, 9, 29, 31, 49, 62; Mr and Mrs R.
Watt, figs 25, 53. The picture research was by Pat
Hodgson.

Contents

Picture Acknowledgments   2
List of Illustrations   4

1 The 1950s   5
2 Early Years, Family and Home Life   14
3 Education and Schools   25
4 Houses, Home Towns and the
    Environment   38
5 Entertainment, Pastimes and Leisure   47
6 The Birth of the Teenager   60

Date List   69
Books for Further Reading   69
Acknowledgments   70
Index   71

The Illustrations

1	Smog in Trafalgar Square	5
2	The tram	6
3	The royal family 1951	7
4	Harold Macmillan	7
5	The Festival of Britain	8
6	The Queen	8
7	A street party for the coronation	9
8	Hillary and Tenzing	10
9	Malayan Independence parade	11
10	Hire Purchase cars	13
11	A maternity clinic	14
12	Woodberry Down Health Centre	16
13	Inside the Health Centre	16
14	Proud parents with pram	17
15	Christmas decorating	17
16	The "hula-hoop"	18
17	An educational toy	18
18	Village grocery	20
19	Grace before school dinner	21
20	Popular selling furniture	22
21	Fashionable furniture	22
22	Girl's bedroom	23
23	Boy's bedroom	23
24	Children in care	24
25	Susie starts school	26
26	Teacher training	27
27	School milk	28
28	Secondary school boys	30
29	On a school trip	31
30	History at Hertford Girls' School	32
31	Kidbrooke housecraft lesson	35
32	Harrow	36
33	School rugby	36
34	Immigrants arrive in London	37
35	A building labourer	38
36	Harlow New Town	39
37	Croxteth shops	40
38	Bethnal Green	41
39	Prefabs	42
40	The last London tram	42
41	A steam train	43
42	Mr Therm presents Gas	44
43	Sainsbury's opening, Eastbourne	45
44	Inside a supermarket	46
45	Dinky Toy coach	47
46	A model garage	48
47	A selection of annuals	50
48	At a junior library	51
49	Davy Crockett	53
50	Watching TV	54
51	Christopher Trace	55
52	Leila Williams	55
53	The new car	57
54	Butlin's campers	58
55	Youth club members	59
56	Bill Haley	61
57	Elvis	62
58	Tommy Steele	63
59	Teddy Boys	64
60	Dancing at a youth club	64
61	Borstal	65
62	Apprentices	66
63	Military Service	67
64	"We all fought a good fight"	68

1 The 1950s

Britain in the early 1950s was only just recovering from the aftermath of a terrible and devastating war. The Second World War had ended in 1945, but there were still shortages of many essential goods and housing; bombsites all around; and a deprived life for many children. Adults feared that the international situation was so tense that, at any moment, the world might be plunged back into the devastation of war. There was hope for the future, and a pride both in the struggles of the war and in the new "welfare state" that had been set up after it; but the fears sometimes outweighed the hopes.

By the end of the 1950s life in Britain had changed in many ways; most people thought, for the better. The war began to seem far behind, with a new world of prosperity opening up for the first time for ordinary people — what people were beginning to call the "affluent society". For

1 Feeding the pigeons in Trafalgar Square — in the smog.

2   The tram, Colwyn Bay.

Until 1952, George VI was king, a much-loved father of his people. He had gained enormous respect during the war, when he and his queen Elizabeth (now the Queen Mother) chose to remain in bombed London and share the suffering of the nation. His death brought the present queen, Elizabeth II, to the throne.

In 1950, the Labour Government, which had been in power since 1945 under Clement Attlee, won another election, but with a greatly reduced majority. The next year, another election brought a Conservative Government to power, under the wartime leader Winston Churchill. The Labour Government had accomplished great things, nationalizing many industries like coal, railways and steel, and establishing a system of social security "from the cradle to the grave", which included the setting-up of improved unemployment provisions and the National Health Service in 1948. But the Government had taken power at a time of enormous economic difficulties, and had been forced to practise a policy of "austerity", telling people they could not have things they wanted, continuing the system of wartime rationing and many wartime restrictions such as having to carry identity cards. The Conservatives won power with their promise to "set the people free" and they were able to introduce the period of mass prosperity. The Conservatives formed the Government throughout the 1950s, increasing their majority at two more general elections, in 1955 and 1959. Winston Churchill was followed as Prime Minister first by Anthony Eden and then by Harold Macmillan.

the first time, large numbers of families had motor cars, televisions and washing machines. Young people suddenly found themselves the possessors of large sums of money to spend and the word "teenager" was invented. There were still fears of war, and the existence of the atom bomb, developed at the end of the Second World War, threatened destruction on an undreamt-of scale. But, as the years passed, people began to learn to live with even this terrible threat, and the possibility of war seemed to recede.

Young people of today would find many things strange if they went back to the early 1950s, even though it is only a relatively short time ago. There were trams and trolley-buses in the streets of the cities; the terrible, blinding fogs called "smogs" sometimes made going out virtually impossible; steam trains still gave people smut in their eyes; and fire engines cleared a path through the roads using no more than bells. By the late 1950s, these things had changed, and many of the things we take for granted today — super-markets, motorways, stereo systems, frozen food — had begun to make their impact.

The Festival of Britain and the Coronation

An event that brightened up British life in 1951, a time when the "age of austerity" had not yet ended and many goods (including sweets) were still rationed, was the Festival of Britain. This huge celebration was held on the devastated South Bank of

6

THE ROYAL FAMILY ON HOLIDAY.—A charmingly informal group, taken in the grounds of Balmoral Castle, with Prince Charles astride a sculptured deer as the centre of attention. The King is holding the handle of Princess Anne's perambulator, and Prince Charles is steadied by his father, the Duke of Edinburgh, while the Queen, Princess Elizabeth and Princess Margaret look on.

PRINCESS CELEBRATES COMING OF AGE

3   A newspaper picture on the occasion of Princess Elizabeth's 21st birthday, August 1951.

4   Harold Macmillan on a drive through Clapham, ➤ London, on his election campaign tour in October 1959.

5   The Dome of Discovery and the Skylon were
built on London's South Bank, especially for the
Festival of Britain in 1951. The festival lasted for
five months.

the river Thames in London, in order to
show people what a better and more prosperous future could hold. The minister in
charge, Herbert Morrison, announced it as
"the people giving themselves a pat on the
back", and £11 million was allocated towards providing "a tonic to the nation"
full of "fun, fantasy and colour". There was
a gigantic funfair, exhibitions showing
Britain's progress in arts and sciences, and
a number of strange buildings like the Dome
of Discovery and the Skylon, a thin, cigar-
like tube towering above the festival ground,
supported in thin air by even thinner cables
(like Britain, some joker said, without visible
means of support). Most of the buildings of
the festival were later pulled down, but the
Royal Festival Hall, London's main concert

6   After her coronation in Westminster Abbey, ➤
the Queen entered the state coach.

8

7 Street parties were held to celebrate the coronation.

hall, is one building that remains from that time. The festival was a great success, visited by over eight million people.

The next great landmark was the coronation of the present Queen, Elizabeth II, in June 1953, the year after the death of her father, George VI. The ceremony in Westminster Abbey was full of the traditional splendour that had marked British coronations for hundreds of years, but this time there was a new element: after some official doubts and misgivings, it was decided that the ceremony should be televised for the first time, and, as a result, millions of the British people and people overseas were able to share in the memorable event. Not many people had television in those days, but people collected together in public places to watch: it was the first time that many children had seen television. Thousands of other people of all ages lined the route from Buckingham Palace to the Abbey, sleeping on the pavements all night before, to be sure of a place, while 30,000 London children had special seats along the route to watch the procession. Millions of children received commemorative mugs to remember the event, and there were street parties. It was all very similar to the Silver Jubilee in 1977 and the Royal Wedding in 1981.

8   Edmund Hillary (second from the left), with sherpa Sen Tenzing behind him, after their triumphant conquest of Everest.

On the morning of the coronation the news came through that Mount Everest, part of the Himalayas range in Nepal and the highest mountain in the world, had at last been conquered by a group of climbers from the British Commonwealth. The two men who actually reached the summit were the New Zealander Edmund Hillary and the local Himalayan guide sherpa Sen Tenzing. This wonderful news seemed to add a special glory to the day of the coronation, emphasizing mankind's achievement and the things of which the human race was capable.

In Britain, life was daily getting more prosperous and easier, and a mood of great optimism developed, summarized by the feeling that Britain was entering "a new Elizabethan age" (a previous age of glory in English history had been the reign of Elizabeth I in the sixteenth century). A special magazine was published to celebrate this new spirit, *The New Elizabethan*, and it

had its junior equivalent, *The Young Elizabethan*, which published a rich mixture of stories, pictures and poetry. Another achievement that caught the imagination of the people, from the world of sport, was the running of the "four minute mile" by the Englishman Roger Bannister in 1954. The attractive young Queen with her popular children, Prince Charles and Princess Anne, in whom the public took great interest, also seemed to symbolize the new spirit. Nowadays, we may view the idea that Britain was entering another Elizabethan age as a little over-optimistic, as there have been many problems since then, especially in the economic sphere. But it was a real feeling at the time, and gave a sense of great excitement to young people growing up in the early 1950s.

Britain and the World: Problems and Achievements

The 1950s may have been an age of growing affluence, but they were also years when international tension and the possibility of another war added a backdrop of fear to ordinary people's lives. After the Second World War ended in 1945, it gradually seemed as if the world had become divided into two hostile blocs of countries, led by the two strongest nations, the United States of America, which believed in the capitalist system, and the Soviet Union, which practised a communist system. Some countries identified themselves wholly with one or other of these powers, while others were non-aligned. Tension between the blocs came to a head with the Korean War in 1950, when there were fears of the war spreading beyond the nations (including the USA and Britain) already involved.

Britain played a different and much greater role in world events in the 1950s than it does now. In the earlier part of the twentieth century it had been one of the world's greatest powers and it was the only country opposed to Hitler's Germany which

had gone through the Second World War from start to finish. It had emerged from the war much weakened and virtually bankrupt, but in the early 1950s Britain was still considered a great power, only a little less important than the United States and the Soviet Union. Britain still had most of its traditional Empire around the world, although there were strong moves towards independence for the colonial people, and the most important of the colonies, India, had already become independen in 1947.

The event that did most to show Britain that it was now a second-class power was the ill-fated Suez adventure of 1956. The Suez Canal was and is an international waterway running through Egypt. This country was formally independent, but had long been dominated by Britain and France, while the Canal was owned and run by an international

9   Many countries of the British Empire celebrated their independence in the 1950s. Here the first elected Supreme Head of State of Malaya watched his troops march past, 1957.

company. In the 1950s Egypt had a new and aggressive nationalist leader, Abdul Gamal Nasser, who quarrelled with Britain and France and nationalized the Canal, sending his troops in to occupy it. Britain and France, incensed by this action and fearing for international trade, sent soldiers in, aided by Israel, which was also threatened by Egypt, demanding that the Egyptians withdraw from the Canal zone. But they soon found that international opinion was very much against this action — especially the opinion of Britain's most important ally, the United States — and the expedition was costing an enormous amount of money. The

11

day after the paratroopers landed in Egypt, the British Prime Minister, Anthony Eden, sent orders to cease fighting. The British and French troops withdrew, to be replaced by a United Nations peacekeeping force. This was a humiliating defeat and demonstrated that Britain's power to act independently in issues of international importance had been seriously weakened.

In the years following the Suez disaster, the process by which Britain dismantled its Empire was speeded up under Harold Macmillan, who succeeded Eden as Prime Minister in 1957. By 1959 Ceylon (now Sri Lanka), Malaya and Ghana were all independent, and rapid moves were underway, to give independence to the nations of Central Africa and the West Indies. What remained of the old Empire were a number of "bases" around the world and some dependencies, mainly countries too small for independence to be feasible. The Empire was replaced by a loose association of nations known as the Commonwealth, but, although many efforts and much goodwill were invested in this, its practical importance was small.

Having lost its Empire, Britain was faced with the problems of finding a new place in the changed world. A great deal of faith was placed in the "special relationship" with the United States and in the formation of the Commonwealth, and, for this reason, when six of the most important nations in Western Europe decided to form the European Economic Community (the "Common Market") in 1958, an economic and trading bloc working for greater co-operation between its member states, Britain decided to stay aloof. It was later to regret this decision, when the EEC countries achieved greater economic progress than Britain, and was eventually to join, but not until the 1970s.

There were many stirring events going on in other parts of the world during the 1950s. In Eastern Europe, the Soviet Union had established its domination over a number of countries, which had their own governments but which were ultimately under Soviet control. In 1956, the Hungarian government and people rose against Soviet domination; but, although the hopes and prayers of many around the world were with them in their struggle for freedom, the revolt ended with the Soviet Union sending its troops into Hungary, and the rising was crushed within a few days. Children growing up in Britain would certainly have heard about this tragic event, which took place at almost exactly the same time as the Suez Crisis.

British children would also have been aware of what was going on in the United States, the most powerful and the richest country in the world, which was building, for the majority of its citizens, the most affluent consumer society the world had seen. The powerful and smooth American car, the limousine, was the great symbol of America in those days. But America also had problems: the desperate poverty that existed in isolated pockets, and the problems of America's black citizens who, especially in the southern states, lacked the most basic civil rights: they could not sit on certain seats on buses or go to the same schools or eating places as white people. There were signs of growing efforts to cope with this problem: the beginning of government action against discrimination, and the campaigns of the inspiring black preacher, Martin Luther King, who advocated mass peaceful resistance as a means of countering oppression.

Other events and people around the world stage included the strong and wise leadership given to West Germany by the aged Karl Adenauer, who helped to heal the wounds of the Nazi past; the election of the much-loved Pope John XXIII in 1958; the birth of the new independent nations in Africa and Asia, which had freed themselves from the rule of the European colonial powers. The 1950s was an age of many problems, but also of great hope and optimism for the future, perhaps more so than now.

A Good Time to Grow Up

Life in Britain in the 1950s has come to appear differently now from the way it appeared at the time. During the 1950s, people were conscious mainly of immense improvements and growing prosperity. These were the years when the car, the television and the refrigerator all entered the average British home — the three essential status symbols of the time for the British family. People became increasingly eager to possess all the modern material goods of the affluent society, and what they could not afford at any one time, they bought on hire-purchase, affectionately nicknamed "the never-never". The Government sometimes tried to restrict the amount of credit available on hire-purchase, but it was the fastest growing social phenomenon of the age. Meanwhile, people dreamed of winning heaps of money on the football pools or on the new Premium Bonds instituted by the Government in 1956, or by becoming one of the new popular entertainers, or that new word at the time, "pop singers". The trade union leader, Ernest Bevin, had once said that British people suffered from "a poverty of desire", but this ceased to be true in the 1950s.

Not surprisingly, with this orgy of acquisitiveness, it was a rather quiet age politically, with few great causes and limited amounts of hatred and resentment. People believed the Conservative Prime Minister, Harold Macmillan, when he told them in 1959 that they "had never had it so good", and so they were content to have the Conservative Governments in power, without much opposition. One commentator noted that the general election of 1955 was the most apathetic Britain had known in the twentieth century so far.

But perhaps the atmosphere of prosperity and ease masked serious problems; and since the 1950s many economic commentators

10   Buying a car on the "never-never", Birmingham, 1956. Unsold vehicles were piling up, and so free trips to Paris were offered to encourage buyers.

have come to believe that the economic problems from which Britain has more recently suffered had their roots in that period. Britain's rate of economic growth, an average of 2.6 per cent per annum, was higher than it had been previously; but it was much lower than the growth rate of Britain's competitors among industrialized nations, such as West Germany and Japan. Their goods increasingly outsold Britain's on world markets and were even preferred increasingly by British consumers. The modern British problems of low productivity and balancing the Government budgets by extensive overseas borrowing also have their roots in the 1950s.

However, children and young people in the 1950s would hardly have been aware of these growing problems. They would probably have been more content with life than British children had ever been: there would have been sweets to eat (after they came off the ration in 1951), a wider choice of toys and books, perhaps a new school to go to, and probably a new, brighter and bigger home than the slums where many British children had once grown up. The 1950s were good years to be young.

13

2 Early Years, Family and Home Life

Birth

The 1950s were years of many innovations in the lives of children and young people, and these began the very moment the child was born. In the late 1940s more than half Britain's babies had been born at home, while many of the children of more well-off parents had been born in private nursing homes. But the new National Health Service, set up in 1948, provided for more hospital places for expectant mothers, and in the 1950s it was increasingly likely that a baby would be born in a hospital: either one of the rather grim old brick buildings that often remained from the Victorian age or one of the new, soaring, glass-and-concrete structures in the architectural style of the age. (Of course, some babies continued to be born at home, and even at the end of the decade, despite some official discouragement, one-third of babies were still being born at home.) The new hospitals were comfortable, and all the resources of modern medical care and training were put into preparing for birth. Under the new National Health Service, health visitors had been appointed to give maternity advice to mothers, and clinics were available for ante-natal classes. But, at the same time as all this science was applied, the 1950s also saw a great new vogue for "natural childbirth", free of the anaesthetics that had been common since Queen Victoria's reign, and of artificial inducements to the birth. All in all, birth was probably a more trouble-free experience for both child and mother than it had ever been.

Child Welfare

This atmosphere of care, protection and concern for health also surrounded the 1950s child in his or her early years, more than it had ever done children in the past. Young children were now taken to child welfare clinics, where their physical progress was checked, where they were given programmes of vaccination against diseases, and where they also received free milk, orange juice and cod-liver oil (the last of these usually regarded with some distaste by its child beneficiaries). Zara Sandler's first baby was born in north London in 1952. Mrs Sandler recalls:

> Very soon after leaving hospital with my first baby, I took her to the local welfare clinic to register her and from then on at

11 A maternity clinic in 1954.

weekly intervals. A health visitor once came to my home to visit me and the baby and when I asked her a question about the type of milk I should use (I wasn't able to feed the baby myself) the health visitor just replied "take her to the clinic" and was never seen again!

During clinic visits the baby was weighed and any general problems discussed either with the paediatrician or a GP.

Vaccination was advised but not insisted upon. One GP who didn't believe in babies crying unnecessarily when they were vaccinated, would pop a chocolate drop into the baby's open mouth and this would alleviate the usual wails and shrieks as the needle was inserted.

Rhys Burriss, who grew up in the 1950s, also remembers the clinic visits:

I especially remember going with my mother to the clinic to be given free orange juice and cod-liver oil. I remember the clinic had a special smell, a sort of "health" smell, unlike anything I'd ever smelt before.
(Rhys Burriss, b. 1951)

A great area of progress during the 1950s was the elimination, often by a programme of vaccinations, of many of the diseases which had threatened child life and caused anguish to parents for many years. Polio was a terrible, crippling disease which had particularly affected children and caused paralysis and even death. But by the mid-1950s a vaccine had been developed against it, which was speedily given to as many children as possible. During the 1950s also, antibiotics were developed which gave protection against tuberculosis, for hundreds of years one of the diseases most feared by adults and children alike. Vaccinations were also now available against other diseases that had often killed children in the past, like diphtheria or whooping cough. All in all, the most serious diseases a 1950s child was liable to suffer became relatively minor complaints such as measles and mumps. The grim "fever hospitals" of the interwar years, which had filled so many children entering them with the terrible fear of being "taken away", became merely a bad memory that adults had.

The improvement in child health was clear from the official statistics. By 1956 the infant death-rate was half that of the immediate pre-war years and had almost reached today's minuscule levels; while the death-rate among mothers giving birth had fallen by 1956 to only one-sixth of what it had been in 1938. In 1950, the Chief Medical Officer of the Department of Education, after examining around two million children, reported that the physical condition of three-and-a-half per cent of them was "poor", but by 1955 the figure had fallen to only one-and-a-half per cent. However, it was not all improvement, and in 1955 as many as 268,000 schoolchildren were reported to be "vermin-infested".

Not only were children of the 1950s in noticeably better health; there were also many more of them. The years immediately after the war until the late 1940s had seen one "baby boom", the result of soldiers coming home to their wives; but another and more sustained boom began in 1955, lasting until the early 1960s. More babies were born in Britain during the 1950s than in any other period in history. During the 1950s the population of Britain increased by some 2.5 million, reaching almost 46 million by the end of the decade, and all these children needed homes and school places. This rise in population was the result of better health care, growing prosperity, and the increasing trend to marry early and have a family (in the early 1950s half the women were married by the age of 25), but it did not mean that families themselves were larger. Throughout the whole of the post-war period, the average size of family has been about 2.2 children, only about half of what it was at the beginning of the century. The family of six, eight or even ten children, which had been quite common in the interwar years and very common before that, now became unusual.

12 New-style architecture for the Woodberry Down Health Centre at Stoke Newington, London.

Children's Clothes

The new prosperity and care were also evident in children's clothes. During the war, when many children had been evacuated from London and other large cities to escape the bombing, the families receiving children from the slum districts had been shocked to find little girls who had never worn knickers under their frocks, and children who had never had coats to wear in winter and had set out on their evacuation journeys wearing only flimsy plimsolls. All that was dramatically changed in the 1950s. The health visitors who came round homes inspecting children were very concerned to see that they were properly clothed; and mothers, who now had more money to spend, took a pride in dressing their children in good shoes and bright poplin dresses and cotton shirts, and giving them varied outfits to wear. Babies were now carried around in the new, sturdy "Princess" prams, which became quite a status symbol for a mother to provide.

Children's clothes and appearance in the

13 Inside the Woodberry Down Health Centre.

14　Proud parents, 1954.

15　Christmas.

1950s differed quite markedly from those of modern children. Little boys always wore short trousers — getting the first pair of long trousers was a real event and a crucial stage on the road to adulthood; they wore short-sleeved shirts (but not tee-shirts) and they always wore vests. Boys (and most men too) almost all wore their hair short, the style known as the "short-back-and-sides". A boy of the 1950s recalls this:

> I remember that when you went to the hairdresser's — or barber's as it was then, some old guy who'd been doing it for years — it was always a "short-back-and-sides". Sometimes they didn't even bother to ask you what you wanted. Or they would say, "Short back and sides?", and you would say "yes". And that was that.
> (Bob Crabtree, b. 1950)

For little girls, poplin and gingham dresses were very popular, and the clothes, like those of older women, came in at the waist. Girls always wore cardigans, not sweaters as boys did. Hair tended to be no more than neck-length, and was often worn with a parting, held by a hair-clip covered with a slide, while fringes were uncommon. One item of clothing, very often worn by girls and since disappeared, was the "liberty bodice":

> Everyone who's my age now will know what a "liberty bodice" was, though maybe girls growing up today won't know. The most accurate way to describe it is that it was a sort of padded vest, similar to boys' vests, but much thicker, and worn in winter, and it was very warm.
> (Penny Williams, b. 1949)

17

16 Doing the "hula-hoop" (see page 49).

17 A toy like this would help the child learn about shapes and sizes.

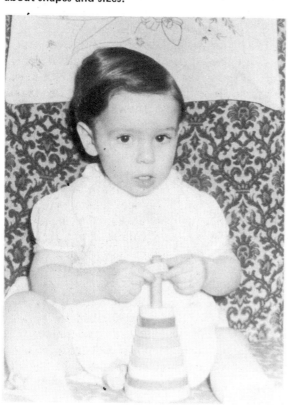

Parents and Children, and Home Discipline

The 1950s saw quite a change in the relations between parents and children, in the direction of a more "child-centred" view and less emphasis on formal discipline. This was by no means entirely new; concern for the child and parents' interest in their children had been growing steadily since the eighteenth century — but the 1950s did see the decisive dropping of certain formal and rigid methods of bringing up small children. In the interwar years, childcare theorists such as Truby King had been very influential. He believed in regular four-hourly feeds, strict potty training, babies who cried between feeds being left alone, and no cuddling. The emphasis was firmly and squarely on not letting the child become spoilt. By the 1950s, a new and immensely powerful influence had taken the place of these ideas — Dr Benjamin Spock, whose book *Baby and Child Care* was first published in the United States in 1947. It was to reach an astonishing worldwide sale of 20 million copies. It was at the height of its influence during the 1950s (published in Britain in 1955), and was backed up by Dr John Bowlby's *Child Care and the Growth of Love* (1953), which gave similar although complementary ideas.

What these two doctors were saying was that the importance of maternal love and of paying attention to the child was greater than the danger of the child being spoilt. Babies from birth needed security, stability and love, and should be given stimulus, educational toys, conversation with adults and comfort when they cried. If children did not want to eat certain foods, or if they persisted in sucking their thumbs, this was nothing to worry about, as the children would probably grow out of it naturally. Dr Spock recommended that a baby should never be left to cry for more than an hour, whereas Truby King had recommended that they should be left to cry until their next feed was due.

The two doctors did differ on certain

matters. Dr Bowlby's great contribution was the theory of maternal deprivation — the idea that the first five years of the child's life are crucial, and that if the constant care and love of the mother are not given during these years, then the child will grow up emotionally crippled and not capable of loving in his or her turn. This meant that mothers should very rarely leave their young children alone, and should not go out to work. Dr Bowlby wrote:

> The mother of young children is not free, or at least should not be free, to earn.

Dr Spock was not quite so certain of this. In a later edition of his book, he recommended that the mother should ask the advice of a social worker before she went out to work. The idea Dr Spock contributed was that the loving care of the father was just as important as that of the mother, and that the two parents should co-operate fully in bringing up the child, where that was possible. In interwar homes the father had sometimes been a rather stern and remote figure, summoned usually when there was a need for the child to be punished, but in the 1950s fathers did grow closer to their children. Fathers even attended the ante-natal classes and began to attend the births of their children, to feed the children and to play with them. The change is evident in the words of one of the Bethnal Green, East London parents interviewed by sociologists Young and Wilmott, in their pioneering study of family life in a working-class district, *Family and Kinship in East London*:

> There's certainly been a change. I whack mine now, but not the beatings like we used to have. When I was a boy most of us feared our fathers more than we liked them. I feared mine and I had plenty of reason to.

Things did not always happen in practice as the two doctors believed they should in theory. Both of them really thought that mothers should stay at home to look after their children — and so did a lot of other people, for the women's liberation movement, which was later to insist on the woman's right to an independent career, was not yet strong in the 1950s. But, even so, the growing wish of women to work and the need of the expanding economy for more workers did mean that more women were going out to work than ever before. In the later 1950s, it was estimated that 3.5 million women were then going out to work. This led to a much-publicized problem of the time, affecting slightly older children — the problem of the "latchkey kids". These were children who let themselves into the house after school when nobody was there — called "latchkey kids" because they often wore the front-door key on a string around their necks. People were more worried by this than they are today, largely because it was a new phenomenon: many people blamed the increase in vandalism and petty crime on unsupervised children who did not go home but roamed the streets instead.

Many other new ideas at the time affected the development of children and their relationship with parents. One of the most important influences (new at the time) was the theory of the child psychologist Jean Piaget, who taught that children's ability to understand the world went through several well-defined stages according to age. For example, the first stage is the *sensory-motor* stage, lasting until the age of two, when the child learns mainly about the nature of objects; and this is followed by the *pre-operational* stage, when the child turns to acquiring a system of language. Piaget's influence led to parents being actively concerned with their child learning properly, and sometimes being careful not to burden it with things it could not understand (or things Piaget said it could not understand). But Piaget's influence, like that of Spock

and Bowlby, did lead towards more "child-centredness", as opposed to the old leave-well-alone approach.

Food

Many other aspects of home life differed in the 1950s from their present pattern — including food. At the beginning of the 1950s shortages were very common, and many essential items of food were still rationed: butter, cheese, bacon, meat, tea and sugar. As the 1950s went on, these items were gradually brought off the ration; the last thing to become freely available was meat, which came off the ration in 1954. But even after that, goods were not available in their present abundance and cheapness, and families ate many types of food which would probably be rather despised today: things like pig's trotters and the heart and brains of sheep. Chicken was then a very expensive meat, and was eaten as a special treat, usually as a Sunday meal.

18   A village grocery in 1953. Notice the bacon slicer and the biscuit boxes.

Food and drink differed then also in that they were more traditional and rather less adventurous. Families ate a lot of stodgy food: bread, potatoes, steak and kidney puddings and pork pies; while lighter dishes, such as salads, were quite rare. Pre-packaged food, so common now, was almost unknown: fish came off the slab, cheese from the board, bacon from the joint, and biscuits were ordered by weight from a large box containing a certain type of biscuit (and, when it was almost empty, the "broken biscuits" were often sold in their turn). Sweets of the time, such as the huge, hard, ball-like sweets called appropriately "gob-stoppers", often came out of jars. Frozen food, like pre-packaged food, was only just beginning to become common at the end of the 1950s. Many cheap and convenient meals of foreign origin which are often eaten today — ham-

20

19 Saying grace before school dinner.

burgers, pizzas, lasagne — were almost unknown in the 1950s. In the late 1950s, more varied food was encouraged by the spread of the new supermarkets, which took to selling what were then viewed as exotic foods: lychees, tagliatelle, champignons, scampi, slab cake — and canned beer or cheap French wine. But all the time, traditional English foods — Robertson's jam, Yorkshire pudding with roast — still retained all their popularity.

Religion

Greater importance was attached to religion in the 1950s than today. The decline in church-going and religious observance, so marked in modern Britain (where only 10 per cent attend services regularly), had already begun in the 1950s, but at that period the majority of children were still being brought up actively as Christians. Family prayers at meals were more common, and children were usually encouraged to say their prayers before going to sleep at night. In the schools, religious teaching was more strict (it was usually called "religious instruction" or even "religious training" rather than "religious education") and in Roman Catholic primary schools, for

instance, it often meant learning the Catechism by heart, with the class repeating it in unison. Church services differed then too: for Roman Catholics, the Mass was still in Latin and conducted according to the Tridentine Rite; for Anglicans, the services were generally Mattins and Evensong rather than services at more varied times, and the Alternative Service Book had not been introduced, all services being conducted according to the 1662 Book of Common Prayer.

Homes

More trivial aspects of the home were different too. Furniture was much more standard then and would look very old-fashioned to us today. There was a great emphasis on curved and highly polished surfaces. Another great trend of the time, which would have affected children more, was the extraordinary boom in keeping caged birds, such as budgerigars and canaries. By 1956 the caged bird population in Britain had reached six million, having multiplied by ten since the end of the war. The budgerigar's "palace" was well-furnished with tilting ladders, mirrors and bells. Keeping tropical fish in aquaria was also popular. Perhaps these animals were so often kept because, on council estates, keeping larger animals was often forbidden, or because so many new homes had been built and people wanted to fill them with life. But the budgie-boom could have its tragedies: distraught children enquiring around the neighbours for a bird which had flown away, or pinning up poignant notices, were a sadly common feature of those years.

We have mentioned some of the many ways in which homes in the 1950s differed from homes today, but there were also ways in which the 1950s set trends which have continued to the present. One of these was that, for the very first time, the majority of British children had a room of their own: a place where they could be private and lead their own life, free from parents, brothers

20 and 21   In 1953 an exhibition was held, called "Register Your Choice". Two identical living rooms were shown, furnished at the same cost, one with popular selling pieces of furniture (fig 20, above) and one with the most fashionable, modern furniture of the time (fig 21, below). The public voted for their choice — the more modern version.

and sisters. This was largely because so many new homes were being built in the 1950s (see Chapter 4, page 38), so that over-crowding became much less, and also because family sizes were smaller. To have their own room was a very great change in the life of children, and would probably have been much envied by the children of the past or of other parts of the world, who often slept four or five to a room or in the same room as their parents. The change was perhaps particularly important for girls, who trad-itionally had a more home-centred life than boys and who could now decorate their rooms with posters, experiment with fashion and make-up and invite their friends in for private chats. Increasingly, now, all children had their own lives, and more and more the whole family met for television-watching, because the television had usually just been introduced and homes only had one, usually in the sitting room (see Chapter 5, page 54).

22　Her own bedroom.

Children Without Parents

A significant minority of children had home lives different from what we have described: children who were without parents or had been separated from them. But the 1950s also saw great improvements in the lives of these children. These stemmed mainly from the Children's Act passed by Parliament in 1948. Before that, children without parents were often in overcrowded homes run by Public Assistance Committees, but some were still in the old workhouses or looked after only by old people. The 1948 Act gave an enlarged children's branch to the Home Office, which for the first time devised an integrated system for helping young persons under 17 who had no parent or guardian.

Under the Act, it became the local autho-rity's duty to appoint a Children's Com-mittee and a Children's Officer. All children without parents, guardians or anyone suitable to look after them were received into care, some living in local authority homes or voluntary organized homes like the

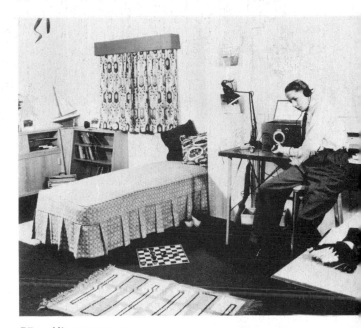

23　His own room.

well-established Dr Barnardo's Homes or the National Children's Home. Great efforts were made to find foster parents for as many of these children as possible, and for very young orphans, adoptive parents might be found. Some of these arrangements must inevitably have been a second best, but the decade could congratulate itself on the humane and responsible steps it had taken to deal with an age-old problem, steps which have continued to the present time. Sadly,

there were still children — runaways or children in homeless families — who escaped the net of the welfare provisions.

24   Teatime for children in care in Middlesex.

The decade also saw important new efforts to help handicapped and maladjusted children, whether the problem was physical or mental. Many special clinics and schools were set up, and there were also large numbers of deaf schools (there are not so many now, because the great progress with deaf aids and modern teaching methods has meant that many children who would once have gone to a deaf school can now attend an ordinary school). In 1959, the Handicapped Pupils and Special Schools Regulations recognized eleven different categories of handicapped children, for all of which different provisions needed to be made. One type of school which was quite common in the early 1950s, but which was less needed later on, was the "health school", provided under the National Health Service for the many children who were delicate because of poor housing, inadequate diet and shortages. These schools, which were built in areas like London's East End, had large, light, airy rooms, large gardens to play in, beds to be used for rest periods and medical staff on hand.

3 Education and Schools

A school student of today going back to the 1950s would find much to recognize but also other things that would seem unfamiliar. The most important date in modern British education is 1944, when the Education Act set in train a complete reorganization of secondary education, and made quite clear the modern distinction between the three stages of education: primary, secondary and further. Before 1944, the education system, while sometimes excellent, was also confusingly organized and patchy in its provision. The beginnings of the modern fully-organized system can be traced back to the late 1940s and 1950s. But there have also been important changes which have taken place since the 1950s. Perhaps most importantly, the great majority of children have come to receive their secondary education in comprehensive schools, rather than under the "tripartite" system set up by the 1944 Act, which provided three different types of secondary school: grammar, secondary modern and technical.

The modern school student might notice that teaching methods were different in the 1950s, with more emphasis on formal learning of rules and note-taking, although noticing this difference would depend on the school; some schools were experimenting with progressive methods in the 1950s, while some schools remain basically traditional in methods in the 1980s.

But perhaps the differences which would be most striking are not in things like organization and methods, but in the actual texture of school life, the feel, smell and look of things. This is the sort of thing one primary school child of the 1950s remembers:

> What I remember are the smells. Desks smelt very strongly, of polish and resin. And books had a special smell then, nothing like modern books, although I can't describe the smell. And I remember the inkwells, because we learnt to write with pen-nibs attached to wooden handles then, and you had to dip it in the inkwell every two or three minutes. There were no ballpoint pens in schools.
> (Bob Crabtree, b. 1950)

A big change occurred in school buildings. The 1950s were great years of rebuilding, and many new schools were being built in modern styles, of glass and concrete, with all modern facilities. Such a school was one of the earliest comprehensive schools, the large school at Kidbrooke, London, opened in 1954 — an immense cluster of crimson, yellow and blue buildings, with 1700 girls, 90 teachers, 5 gymnasia and a radio control room (the *News Chronicle* thought it was a "palace of learning", while the *Evening Standard* called it a "sausage machine"). There was a great drive to build new schools in the early 1950s, partly to replace the 5,000 schools that had been damaged in air-raids during the war, and 2,000 had been built by 1952, but very many schools remained from the Victorian and Edwardian ages, with their dark brick, small windows and grim yards enclosed by walls (some of them, indeed, remain today).

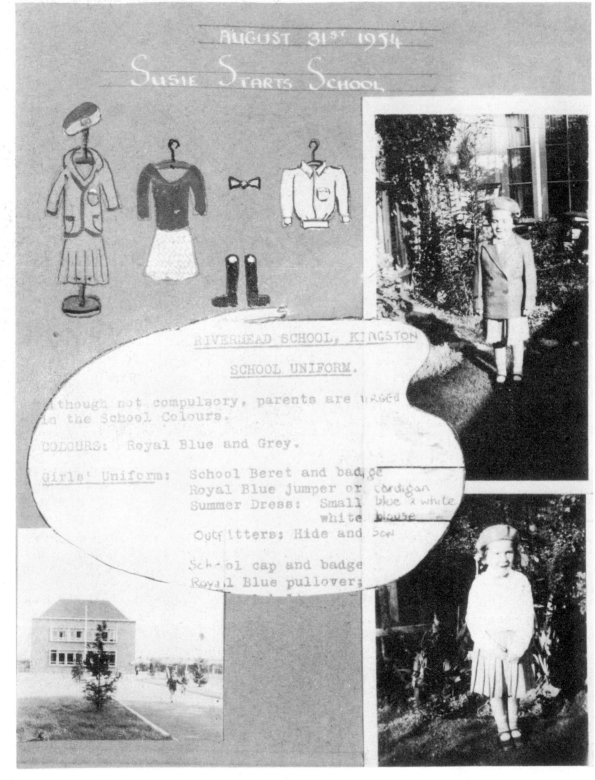

AUGUST 31st 1954

Susie Starts School

RIVERHEAD SCHOOL, KINGSTON

SCHOOL UNIFORM.

Although not compulsory, parents are urged
in the School Colours.

COLOURS: Royal Blue and Grey.

Girls' Uniform: School Beret and badge
                   Royal Blue jumper or cardigan
                   Summer Dress: Small blue & white
                                  white blouse

                   Outfitters: Hide and Son

                   School cap and badge
                   Royal Blue pullover;

But the need for new school buildings was so great that it often could not be met immediately. This led to the need for a frequent feature of the 1950s school landscape: huts. The school leaving age had been raised from fourteen to fifteen in 1947, and to cope with the extra pupils, hordes of concrete H.O.R.S.A. (hutting operation for the raising of the school-leaving age) began to rise in the playgrounds, on the wastelands and amid the weeds of the flowering bombsites. During the 1950s, the number of children needing to be educated was so great that most schools had these huts, and it was very common for small children to begin their education at age five in huts, and move on to the main school later.

The expansion of the school population also meant there was a crying need for more teachers, and a massive teacher-training operation was set in motion in the late 1940s and 1950s, often for people who had been in the services during the war. This generation of teachers has become a legend in the teaching profession, for its enthusiasm and dedication. All in all, with new teachers, buildings and methods, the 1950s were exciting years for British education, when a good education was provided for large numbers rather than for just the privileged few as it had been in the past.

Primary Schools

Some of the changes that we have been describing could be well seen in primary schools. It was in primary schools that the most progress was made towards a freer and more flexible curriculum, because the pressure of examinations at the primary level (at least, in the earlier stages) was not so great. But the buildings and equipment in the primary sector tended to be the older ones, because the school building programme after 1945 favoured secondary schools. By the end of the 1950s not many more than half of the nation's primary schoolchildren were being taught in post-war buildings.

26 A teacher training college. Accommodation was scarce, and so students often had to sit on the floor.

Children usually came to the primary schools at the age of five, with no experience of learning outside the home. The 1944 Education Act had recommended that nursery schools be built for children to attend before school, but, as we have said, in the 1950s, it was usually believed that children should stay with their mother in the home, and nursery school provision then was even more inadequate than it is now. To compensate for this a little, the age of starting school was usually slightly more flexible than it is today, and it was not unknown,

27

especially in country districts, for children to begin school soon after they were four, if they could already read or were thought to be ready for school.

As we have said, in the 1950s, experiments in education were strongest in the primary sector. There were moves in many schools towards setting up an "integrated day", instead of dividing up the lessons into periods, and towards developing "open-plan classrooms", where pupils could learn at their own pace and even move between classrooms if they wanted to. Some areas of education were changing rapidly during the decade: at its beginning, mathematics and arithmetic teaching depended a lot on mental arithmetic problems, "sums", and the chanting of multiplication tables in unison, but by the late 1950s, the "new mathematics" had begun to be popular, with the emphasis on teaching children to understand the *ideas* behind mathematics through the use of examples, projects and structures. In the early 1950s great emphasis was laid on the formal and early learning of reading

skills, often taught by means of the *Janet and John* books, which were introduced in 1951, but by the end of the decade there was more interest in experiment, with a freer attitude, and the use of methods like the "initial teaching alphabet", which was introduced in 1959. Many people welcomed these new approaches, but others feared that they would lower reading standards and lead to more children leaving school illiterate.

In matters of discipline, primary schools led in the new "child-centred" approach. Traditional methods of discipline for younger children, such as keeping them quiet by making them hold their fingers to their lips, were still very common, and the cane was still used on very young children. But, in general, the emphasis was squarely on the need to understand and care for children: the influence of Doctor Spock carried on from the home to the school, while the influence of the child development theorist

28

Piaget was even stronger in schools than it was in homes.

One way in which primary education differed greatly in the 1950s from today was that the later stages of it were dominated by preparation for the "eleven plus". This examination had been set up under the 1944 Education Act, to determine which type of secondary school a child should go to: a grammar school or a secondary modern school. Those who passed the examination were offered grammar school places (this differed from the situation before 1944, when many grammar school places were open to people who paid fees, while others were offered on the basis of competitive scholarships). Great emphasis was placed on the "eleven-plus" examination, since many parents believed it was immensely important that their child got a grammar school education and would not have wished to send their child to a secondary modern. Some parents started scheming to get their child into the local grammar school almost from the moment of birth, and, as the examination approached, many young children were placed under enormous strain; one commentator at the time described it as "an annual pitched battle of childish wits and nerves". Eleven-plus cramming books poured from the publishing houses, and many children were given special lessons from private tutors to help them to pass. Proposals that the examination might be replaced by a system of teachers' assessment were not carried out, because it was feared that the teachers might be attacked or driven out of town by parents whose children had not been given a grammar school place. More stress was added to the system by the fact that there were more and larger grammar schools in some areas than in others, so that a child's chance of getting a place partly depended on where he or she lived. Whatever the merits of the grammar and secondary modern schools compared with modern comprehensive

schools, it must surely be something to be thankful for that young children are no longer exposed to such a system of selection.

Secondary Schools: the New System

It was to the secondary school system that the Education Act of 1944 made the most difference. It introduced, for the first time, a unified system of secondary education covering the whole nation. In 1938 37 per cent of all pupils in the state educational system were receiving their whole education in "all-age schools", which they usually left at the age of fourteen, the official school-leaving age. There were already some modern and central schools (which were to develop into the later secondary moderns) and also grammar schools, where large numbers of children could go, paying fees. The 1944 Act changed this system radically. It recommended that a clear distinction should be made between primary education (until age eleven) and secondary education (where it provided that the school leaving age should be raised — in 1947 it became fifteen). The local authorities were required to provide as many secondary schools as necessary in their locality, but the Act did not specify what types of secondary schools were necessary, merely stating that schools should be provided "suitable to different ages, abilities and aptitudes". In practice, this meant the "tripartite" system of grammar, secondary modern and technical schools (but chiefly the first two of these).

This reorganization, however, took place in the wake of wartime disruption, and it took time to implement, so that some of the old features survived, despite official disapproval. Thus, during the early 1950s there were still more than one million children attending the "all-age schools", which in theory had been abolished, although by the end of the decade they had virtually died out. Similarly, at the primary level, there was now meant to be a maximum of 30

28   Secondary school boys, 1958.

pupils in a class, but because of the large numbers of children and the shortage of teachers, classes of up to 40 primary school children were not uncommon throughout the 1950s and into the 1960s.

During the 1950s, there were a large number of types of secondary school in existence, because as well as the three types of the "tripartite" system, the first comprehensive schools were being opened, although there were not yet many of them. Like today, there were also the small minority of schoolchildren being educated at public schools (schools outside the state education system). We shall now look at the different kinds of school in turn.

The Secondary Modern Schools

The secondary modern schools were controversial in the 1950s. Many of them were centres for new ideas and gave an excellent, practical-style education. But many people also considered that secondary moderns were inferior: this was, after all, where the eleven-plus failures went, and many of them were the same schools as the old modern or "all-age" schools, which had previously given a very inferior education for working-class children. Middle-class parents still did not want to send their children to a secondary modern, and the historian A. J. P. Taylor was only voicing the feelings of many people when he said that young people should "run away to sea rather than go to a secondary modern".

30

It was sad that some of the bad publicity undermined the good work that many secondary modern schools were doing. It was these schools that pioneered the "project" method of learning, which has since become much more common. Practical finding-out was encouraged by ideas like visiting commerce and industry, inviting speakers from different walks of life to come into the schools to talk about their work, and adopting farms. The secondary moderns also developed the practice of the school trip abroad, and soon, English children were a common sight in Dieppe, Boulogne and the other ports of north France (the more far-flung school trip had to wait until the more affluent 1960s).

The secondary moderns also tried hard to counteract the image of being a place where failures went, and were soon encouraging their students to stay on at school and take examinations. The General Certificate of Education (G.C.E.) had been launched in

1951: this examination, where students gained passes in a number of subjects, replaced the old School Certificate, where a certificate was only awarded if the candidate passed in at least five subjects, which had to include English, a language, mathematics or a science, and also reached a general good standard in the examination as a whole. At first, it was intended that the new examination should only be taken at age 16, which would effectively have barred secondary modern students, as they usually left at the official leaving age of 15. The thinking behind this idea was that it was better that the secondary moderns should concentrate on practical-style teaching, without the distraction of examinations. But, in 1953, the rules were changed, to allow the examination to be taken at a younger age, and soon, large numbers of secondary modern were offering GCE courses. There was also a marked trend for students to stay on beyond the school leaving age to get more qualifications: 9,000 had done so in 1947, but by 1957 the figure was 21,000. But an alternative system of examination to the G.C.E, the Certificate

29   Girls with duffle bags on their way to a skiing holiday.

of Secondary Education (C.S.E.) was not available during the 1950s, being announced in 1963.

However, it would be idle to pretend that there were not problems with the secondary moderns. They suffered from a very high turnover of staff, were often situated in slum areas, which gave rise to problems of discipline and crime, and could not shake off continuing bad publicity. A secondary modern schoolboy of the late 1950s, interviewed for Peter Willmott's study *Adolescent Boys of East London*, expressed the feeling that he did not get the utmost from school:

I wish I'd got somewhere when I was at school. I can see my mistake now, but I didn't know what school meant at the time. I didn't realize about GCEs and all that — I can see now that you're much better off if you can stay at school a bit

30   A history lesson for the Upper 4th, The Girls' School, Hertford, 1953.

longer and sit GCEs. But at my school there was only about one person in fifty who did GCEs.

Many young people left these schools with a pervasive sense of failure and of never having been given a chance, and it was largely the feeling that the country was condemning the majority of its children to a permanent second-class life at the early age of eleven which led to demands (ultimately carried out) that a comprehensive system of education be introduced, providing schools where all children could be educated.

The Grammar Schools
During the 1950s the grammar schools educated the approximately 20 per cent of

the nation's children who had passed the eleven-plus. The grammar schools were ancient institutions, some of them dating back hundreds of years, which prided themselves on their traditions and on the excellent academic education that they gave their pupils. The 1944 Act had brought great changes to the grammar schools, giving them a choice between taking all their pupils free and accepting the pupils chosen by the education authorities, or going outside the state education system entirely and becoming independent. (A small minority of schools, known as the "direct grant" schools, reached a compromise where 25 per cent of the students were taken free, while the rest paid fees).

This move towards taking the pupils free and solely on the basis of the eleven-plus examination brought great changes to the grammar schools. Before the war the grammar schools had taken very few children from working-class backgrounds, and only 14 per cent of children had continued their education beyond the age of fourteen. But by the 1950s one-half of the children in grammar schools were the children of manual workers, with skilled workers' children being an especially strong element. Many of these children got the sort of chances to go on to universities and in to the professions that they would never have had before, and this expansion of social opportunity was the grammar schools' great achievement. If it was the sense of failure and waste associated with the secondary moderns that prompted those who wanted to change over to a comprehensive system, it was the academic excellence and educational opportunities offered by the grammar schools that motivated those who wanted things to stay as they were.

However, the social expansion of the grammar schools was not without its well-publicized problems. Boys and girls from working-class backgrounds sometimes found that the move to the grammar school set up a conflict between the demands of school and the expectations of home life. They might become separated from their friends who had gone to secondary modern schools, and they might find that parents, who had not themselves had educational opportunities, did not understand or feel in sympathy with the demands for academic work that the school made. Here are the words of one grammar school boy of the late 1950s, interviewed in *Adolescent Boys of East London*:

My parents took no interest in my school. They didn't like me doing homework at all; they thought you shouldn't be doing it in your own time. I used to take up a whole table every night with homework. They thought there was a time for work and a time for play. You got no encouragement. They'd look at the report at the end of the term and that was about it. They didn't seem to realize what education meant.

This boy left grammar school, worn out with the pressures, at the age of 15. He was by no means untypical: of the boys in this survey who left grammar school, nearly a third had left at 15, and nine out of ten before the age of 17. This problem of the "early leavers" was exacerbated, when the grammar school boys saw their friends from secondary moderns already out at work and earning good wages. These boys often encouraged them to leave in their turn. Another grammar school boy interviewed in the study said:

They went to work, they made their way in the world, and you were still at school and they thought of you as a kind of low life. They almost regarded you as a cissy. Possibly the reason for that is that deep down they resented the fact that you still went to school. . .

These were the attitudes of some: other

students (and their parents) appreciated and were willing to take advantage of the opportunities they had been given. Another East London grammar school boy said:

You get a chance to ask questions at school and to find out for yourself. I assume I've got some intelligence, and the school can help you to use it — I got seven "O"-levels and I'm now preparing for my "A"-levels. I think the school has given me a broader outlook on life as well — more of an appreciation of different things. And because of having a higher education, I can talk to all sorts of people.

The grammar schools were also adapting their teaching methods and curriculum during the 1950s, although they did not use the "project-based" study of the secondary moderns. Before the war, they had laid a great deal of emphasis on the study of Latin and Greek and on humanities subjects, but rather neglected science subjects, but the balance was redressed in the 1950s: by the end of the decade 60 per cent of the students in the grammar school sixth forms were following science-based courses. However, in most ways, the grammar schools remained traditional in their attitudes: they were largely single-sex schools, and they continued above all to lay stress on academic excellence, with lists on the walls of former headmasters and students who had won scholarships to universities.

The grammar school training was academic, and other activities were subordinated to this, but they did encourage students to take part in out-of-school activities which had educational value: activities like drama, music, badminton and the School Association. Music in schools made giant strides in the 1950s, and students were often now able to carry their interest beyond the school into the wider world: the National Youth Orchestra was founded in the 1950s, and there were organizations such

as "Youth and Music", founded by Sir Robert and Lady Mayer, which enabled young people to attend musical events and concerts cheaply and to give hospitality to young musicians from abroad.

Technical Schools
The third part of the tripartite system was meant to be schools offering education to students with a marked technical ability and aptitude, but this was always the weakest part of the system, and eventually it died out altogether, largely of its own accord. Before the war there had been junior technical colleges and trade schools, and the 1944 Act assumed that this sector of education would continue to expand, but it left the actual implementation to the local authorities. But after the war the local authorities built only 64 of these schools.

This part of the system failed for a number of reasons. First, both grammar schools and secondary moderns were rapidly expanding their science departments during the 1950s, so it began to be questioned whether there was any need for special schools concentrating on science and technology. Secondly, the technical schools did not usually take pupils until the age of 12 or 13, and by this time many of the students who would have benefited from a technical education had taken up grammar school places, where they concentrated on the expanding science courses. Also, the technical schools suffered from a shortage of skilled teachers and often had poor premises, sometimes sharing with technical colleges, which themselves had inadequate facilities.

The Development of Comprehensive Schools
When the tripartite system was set up after 1944, there were already doubts about classifying children into different types at the age of eleven, and the earliest demands were heard for a system of education which would take all types of children, regardless of levels of ability. Several local authorities,

including the London County Council, committed themselves in theory to a comprehensive system of education, but it was not until the early 1950s that the earliest comprehensives were opened. They appeared in some cities, and also in isolated rural areas, where the need to collect students together from over a wide area made them the most practical type of school: by the mid-1950s areas such as the Isle of Man, Anglesey and parts of central Wales had fully comprehensive systems. By the end of the 1950s there were about 100 comprehensive schools in England and Wales, but they still catered only for a small minority of school students. This was because the Labour Party, when it was in power in the early 1950s, did not yet fully back comprehensive education, and after that the Conservative Party, which generally believed in the virtues of the system as it was, was in power for many years. It was only when the move towards comprehensivization had the full backing of Labour Governments after the 1950s that the system made rapid progress and reduced other types of schools to a small minority.

The new comprehensives differed markedly from other schools of the time. Their buildings, especially in city areas, tended to be new, and they were usually very large schools (up to 2,000 pupils rapidly became a norm), because it was felt that only this number could guarantee the full range of courses they wanted to offer, and ensure that they had sixth-forms of adequate size. The early comprehensives, like many other schools of the time, were often single-sex schools, but, in other ways, they mirrored modern trends: they were equipped with up-to-date facilities, and it was these schools that tended to make the experiments, in areas like less structured teaching methods and more pupil democracy, that were to become more common in the 1690s. Various schools in different parts of the country became quite famous for these sorts of experiments.

31 A housecraft lesson at Kidbrooke Comprehensive School for Girls, a "palace of learning", according to the *News Chronicle*.

The Public Schools

The public schools (private schools taking in students whose parents paid fees) were ancient institutions, many of them dating back hundreds of years, and in the 1950s they continued to provide a traditional and privileged education to a small minority, although, like other schools at the time, they were changing. Before 1957 they were largely unregulated by the state, and some of the smaller preparatory schools for younger boys were of very dubious standards, but in that year Department of Education Inspection was introduced, which led to improvements where schools were weak. The public schools during the 1950s were almost entirely single-sex institutions (with the schools for boys being much more

32   A class at Harrow, public school.

33   A school match, between Dulwich (at home) and St Paul's, 1950.

famous. The ceremonies and methods of discipline which had been the stuff of public school boys' stories for a hundred years sometimes continued — at Eton during the 1950s the birch, administered on the traditional flogging block, continued in use, being eventually substituted by the cane — although modern ideas were gradually percolating through. The public schools were very popular with parents in the 1950s, with the longest waiting lists in their history, largely because the grammar schools had become much more socially mixed and there was a market for schools that remained socially exclusive. The extra fees produced by this, and generous grants from business bodies, were often used to build splendid new laboratories for the schools, to satisfy the growing demand for science teaching that was being felt in all sectors of the education system.

Children with Foreign-Born Parents

Children in Britain in the 1950s were increasingly likely to have parents who had been born abroad. Immigration into Britain was by no means new (the large-scale Irish immigration had begun in the 1830s and 1840s, and Jewish immigration from the 1880s and 1890s), but from the 1930s onwards new groups began to arrive. The disasters of war and persecution in Europe accounted for the coming of large numbers of Jews, Poles, Greek Cypriots and Spaniards, while other people from Europe came seeking work. Also, from the 1950s onwards, large numbers of British citizens arrived from Commonwealth countries, and especially the West Indies, hoping for a more prosperous and better life for themselves and their children but sometimes facing hostility and prejudice from longer-established groups.

Growing up in the 1950s for children of foreign-born parents had its special features. Often, these groups congregated in certain areas, and there might be children whose first language was not English, which could lead to a certain isolation from British life, although children and young people obviously found it easier to integrate than sometimes their parents did. The children of European immigrants often tended to go to Roman Catholic schools, although here they were able to mix with a variety of people which led to successful integration. Already in the 1950s some schools had begun to make arrangements for special teaching of students whose first language was not English, although large-scale programmes for multi-cultural education did not yet exist.

The coming of many foreign-born people to Britain in these years was just one aspect of a process by which Britain, for many generations a rather insular and inward-looking country, began to receive more foreign influences. This process affected

34   Victoria Station, June 1956.

growing up in many ways, from the fashion for teenagers to wear Italian-style suits and listen to American pop music, to there being an increasing variety of dishes eaten in the home, to the spread of more easy and relaxed manners than British people had traditionally had. There were some fears that native traditions might be weakened, but, counteracting this, was a richness and liveliness accepted by the young as part of their heritage.

4 Houses, Home Towns and the Environment

During the 1950s, the need to rebuild after the destruction of the war, the expansion of the economy and the drive to give all British citizens a decent home all combined to unleash one of the greatest waves of building Britain had ever seen. Over larger and larger areas a new landscape came into being: great blocks of flats and hundreds of identical office buildings, petrol-fumed motor roads, public lights, advertisements, filling stations, pylons, traffic-lights. It was a new landscape very similar in many ways to those appearing in Europe and North America, and so the traditional character of the regions was minimized as the tide of mass prosperity swept through them all.

Perhaps the most obvious way in which the great wave of building and redevelopment would have affected the young would have been in changing the home they lived in. The war had ended with a great housing shortage, with many houses destroyed and other families living in desperately overcrowded conditions or in slums. But both Labour and Conservative Governments set up a great "housing drive" in their turn, and by 1956 about two-and-a-half million new houses had been built since the war's end. By the end of the decade one family in every five had moved into a newly-built home during the decade. Young people growing up now are more likely to live in a home built in the 1950s than in any other decade.

Most people were pleased that they had acquired good, modern homes. It was not all change: by the end of the decade more than three million families were still living in homes officially classified as slums, and, especially in the north of England, very many of the old two-up two-down back-to-back houses dating from the last century still remained. During most of the decade, about two families in every five were still in the six great city areas or "conurbations" spread over Britain, but more and more families were moving out to the "new towns" and the suburban housing estates. Here they gained a house of their own, more light, fresh air and space and an improved environ-

35   **A building labourer loading breeze blocks to build walls for houses, November 1950.**

ment generally, although some missed the cheerful bustle and dirt of the old city streets.

And it was not all gains in the environment. Despite all the efforts of modern governments, there have probably been ways in which the environment has been rapidly deteriorating. The 1950s saw the beginning of the fashion for building high-rise flats, and these have caused many problems. The motor car, which first became common in Britain during the 1950s, has brought much new freedom to families, but has also greatly increased pollution from noise and fumes, reduced the space where children can play, made large areas unsafe for them and sometimes, if pollution becomes intense, poses a threat to their health. The demands of traffic have probably had the worst effect on children living in cities. Before the 1950s, moving around the city, on foot or by bicycle, was easy and safe for the urban child, as there were only simple double-lane roads. But the new traffic systems built since the 1950s to cope with increasing traffic — the roundabouts, the multi-lane circulation systems, the flyovers — have set up a whole series of barriers to the child moving far from his or her home, and mothers have become reluctant to let children ride on cycles round city streets. Most areas of life for the 1950s child were improving, but it became clear that there was sometimes a price to pay.

The New Homes and Towns

The 1950s saw the British people trekking out of the crowded cities that had been their customary environment for so long into a world which mixed city and country life in a new way. A new type of environment for growing up in was appearing in the 1950s — the "new town". The idea of planned towns sited in rural areas, to relieve the congestion of the cities, was a relatively new one, having been given official sanction by the system of town and country planning set up after the war. New towns were built around many of Britain's cities, but especially around London, where a ring of them was rapidly developed — Basildon, Stevenage, Harlow, Crawley. A place like Crawley, only a village at the start of the decade, had by the end of the 1950s, become a town of more than 60,000 people.

36   Harlow New Town takes shape.

37 Croxteth shops.

Other towns in south-east England, which had already existed, had new housing estates built at their edges, to take on London's "overspill" population, the people who had been living in overcrowded conditions and slums in areas such as the East End and other parts of inner London. The Londoners, naturally, had mixed feelings sometimes about leaving their native environment, but, when they did decide to move, it was usually because they wanted to give their children a better and cleaner life than was possible in the dirty and often vermin-infested older houses. One East End woman, interviewed in Young and Willmott's study *Family and Kinship in East London*, talks about why the family decided to move from Bethnal Green in the East End to the new housing estate in Essex:

We came to Greenleigh for Bill's sake. He was very ill with diphtheria. He got it by drinking the drain water from the sinks of the two families living above us. On top of that he was born bronchial. It has done the boy good to be out here.

Parents who often missed family and neighbours still living in the cities rejoiced at their children's pleasure in parks, gardens and colourful new shopping centres and in the bright new schools they went to. The new environment was, in some ways, less lively than the one they had come from — the trim self-service stores at the centre of the estate replaced the corner shops, the street barrows and the cries of costermongers — and people could feel very isolated, with single families of just parents and children split away from the broader family and the neighbours, whose house and facilities they had shared. But the gains in terms of sanitation, cleanliness and privacy were very great, and, over time, the new towns built up their own community life to replace what had been lost.

The 1950s also saw the development of another new type of home, less desirable than the new town houses: this was the high-rise flat-block. Some people had continued to live in the inner city areas, and when the slums were pulled down here, it was usually believed to be cheaper, more economical of space and more fashionable to rehouse the slum dwellers in high-rise flats, in blocks of up to 17 storeys. Some of the earliest estates built, such as the Alton Estate at Roehampton, were regarded as architectural triumphs in their own time, and some of the high-rise blocks were liked by the people who moved into them; but it soon became clear that many of the more cheaply-built blocks, built by local councils, would quickly suffer problems of deterioration and were likely to have paper-thin walls, inadequate sanitation systems, damp, malfunctioning lifts and so on. Moreover, it was gradually realized that the high-rise flat was an unsuitable environment for a child, who was deprived of a street or garden to play in, and was often kept in by his or her mother, who feared the danger from heights and the crime and violence that often became endemic in these blocks. Children began to find ways of adapting themselves to the flats — inventing games like chasing each other up and down the lifts — but, all too often, their frustration began to be expressed in the growing problem of vandalism among the young. This was a problem that began in the 1950s and was to grow worse in the 1960s, until families with children began to be moved out of the high-rise blocks.

Everywhere, the new homes, houses or flats, were being built — but not quickly enough, for most of the 1950s, to solve the housing shortage. Another characteristic type of dwelling was the "pre-fab" (short for pre-fabricated), which was often put up on bombsites. The walls, made from asbestos sheets, and temporary fittings were simply assembled on the site. The "pre-fabs" were only meant to last families a few years until a new home was built for them. But thousands of families continued to live in them throughout the 1950s and for years afterwards, and there are still a few remaining examples today.

All this emphasis on new types of homes may have given the impression that the 1950s were years of constant uprooting for the young, but this would be a false impression. Before the war, most families had lived in houses rented to them by private landlords, a system which encouraged more frequent moves. It was not uncommon for children growing up then to live in ten different houses during their childhood and

38   Children in Bethnal Green, 1954.

youth. But, by the 1950s, private renting had started a rapid decline, and all the new homes built were either bought by their occupants or rented to them by local authorities: in both cases, once a family had moved into the new home, they tended to stay there. More 1950s children than children ever before enjoyed the benefits of a stable home, school and circle of friends.

The Changing Environment

Many other changes in the everyday scene would have been noted by the 1950s child. Many of them were connected with changing patterns of transport. In 1952 there were still only 2,762,000 private cars on the road, and both the roundabout and the traffic-light were sights noted for their rarity; the most common sight at traffic junctions in busy cities was the policeman, with arm up-raised, on point-duty. By the end of the decade, the number of private cars had more

39   Prefabs in Gretna Green, 1956.

40   The last London Tram pulls into New Cross Garage, 5 July 1952.

than doubled, and great new roads were just one new method of coping with them. Britain's first eight-and-a-half mile stretch of motorway was laid in 1958 and the M1 was opened in 1959.

Public transport was changing fast too. The first week of July 1952 was "last tram week" in London, and there were emotional crowd scenes when the last tram of all drew into New Cross Garage on July 5. Trams continued for rather longer in other cities, and throughout most of the 1950s there were trolleybuses (powered from overhead, not ground, rails). The 1950s also saw the phasing out of steam trains, and this, together with the closing of the country branch lines that was soon to come, ensured that never again would train spotting be the exciting experience it had been for generations of British "railway children", waiting in lonely vantage-points for the distant puff of smoke on the horizon.

Other traditional wonders of childhood were vanishing too. For centuries, a memorable, if sometimes frightening, part of a city childhood had been the paralysing "smogs", when everything was shrouded in a sooty mist and it was difficult to see further than your hand. A character in a novel by Evelyn Waugh had once traced the distinctive quality of English life back to fog:

> We had a foggy habit of life and a rich, obscure, choking literature . . . .Out of a fog we could rule . . . .
> We designed a city that was meant to be seen in a fog.

1952 was the year of the last great "pea-souper" in London, when people groped their way home wearing masks, and thousands died from bronchitis. Soon afterwards, a Clean Air Act was passed which allowed only smokeless fuels, such as coke, to be burned, and, as if miraculously, the age-old phenomenon of "smog" ended. The coming-into-being of a new, clean atmos-

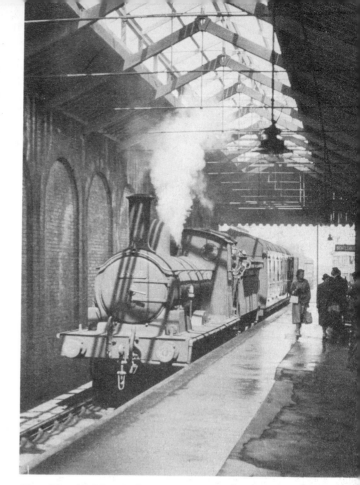

41   The 12.30 train from Saxmundham arrives at Aldeburgh, Suffolk, 1953. The line is now closed.

phere seemed to parallel the replacement of the old, looming dark-brick buildings in cities like London by the gleaming new structures in glass and concrete. Britain was certainly much cleaner and brighter, but had it lost something of the character that made it what it was?

Bombsites were another common sight of the 1950s, many of them blooming with flowers and shrubs in a marvellously natural way and turned by the 1950s young into some of the first "adventure playgrounds". Other places which children loved, around the growing new towns and housing estates, were the woods and wild places which had not yet been developed for housing. They often contained ponds and lakes where

CURTAIN UP ON Mr. THERM
at the Festival

While Britain is at home to the world, Mr. Therm — Britain's gas industry personified — is lending a helping hand everywhere . . . just as usual. Gas, for example, is taking care of the heating and cooking in the fine new Royal Festival Hall, and Mr. Therm is very busy in the kitchens serving the South Bank exhibition restaurants. Gas, too, has had an important part in the making of many of the exhibits. All over Britain, gas makes things easier in the home, and provides the plentiful hot water essential for healthy conditions where food is prepared and handled. And the use of gas and its companion fuel, coke, helps to get rid of fog, for both are smokeless. Besides gas and coke, gas-making produces many valuable synthetic products from coal — drugs, dyes, plastics, fertilisers and many more, of the greatest use to all of us.

So please accept a welcome from Mr. Therm. You'll find that he's helping you, in all sorts of unexpected ways, all over Britain . . . .

GAS AT YOUR SERVICE

ISSUED BY THE GAS COUNCIL

fishing and tadpoling were possible.

In the streets of towns, too, things were changing. In the early 1950s there were no supermarkets. The main types of large store existing then were department stores, but a visit to one of these was generally a rare treat for a child. Much more common was the experience of the innumerable corner shops, usually visited three or four times a week because there was no frozen food then. A boy of the 1950s remembers what made them special:

◄ **42   Before the Clean Air Act, the Gas Council was advertising gas "to get rid of fog". Mr Therm was a well-known character from the Gas Council.**

43   25 February 1952 — opening day at Sainsbury's self-service shop at 31 Terminus Road, Eastbourne.

The corner shops of those days sold everything, from sweets to paraffin. They were hardware shops, newsagents, fruit, vegetable and flower shops all rolled up into one. Entirely different from modern corner shops, which are really mainly grocer's shops. (Bob Crabtree, b. 1950)

The appearance since the 1950s of large supermarkets and shopping developments has largely killed off many of the traditional types of shops that existed then: haberdashers, hatters, fishmongers. It also seems to have taken away some of the distinct-

45

44   The new supermarket at Maidenhead, 1955.

iveness of shops and their special signs. In
the 1950s, you could still identify a barber's
shop from the pole outside and a chemist's
by the differently-coloured jars in the
window. But the early supermarkets, when
they appeared in the late 1950s (in 1947
there had been only ten self-service stores
in Britain, but by 1956 they were being
opened at the rate of 50 a month), must
have been exciting for a child: all the things
that are familiar now — the trolleys and
metal baskets, the endless shelves, the great
variety of goods, the check-outs — would
have been entirely new and different to a
child of the 1950s.

5 Entertainment, Pastimes and Leisure

Toys and Games

The urge and need for children to play with toys is ancient, and many of the types of toys played with by children in the 1950s — dolls and dolls' houses, teddy bears, model trains — went back a hundred years or far into history. During the war there had been a marked shortage of toys, and, although there was much more quantity and variety of toys in the 1950s, the sophisticated electronic and highly elaborate toys of today were still far in the future. The train sets were now starting to be electric, how-

45 A new Dinky toy reflecting new fashions in summer holidays.

New this month!

DINKY TOYS No. 283 **B.O.A.C. Coach**

All air travellers are familiar with the coaches that carry passengers to and from the Airports, and will readily recognise this accurately-detailed model of a B.O.A.C. Coach on Commer chassis. It is correctly finished in blue and white with B.O.A.C. name and symbol on the sides. Fitted with rubber tyres. Length: 4¾″ Price 4/3 each (inc. tax)

46   A model garage with different kinds of vehicles, on sale in 1953.

ever, while the model cars, usually known as "Dinky toys", which had been first introduced in 1933, became even more popular and colourful now that many families actually owned a real car. The "matchbox toys", model cars so small that they could fit inside a matchbox, were also highly popular in the 1950s, although they are viewed as too unsophisticated by the young today.

There were some new toys in the 1950s, however — especially new dolls for girls (the doll for boys, such as "Action Man", had not yet been invented). The 1950s saw a vogue for more realistic dolls: for younger girls, there were baby dolls who wet themselves, while for slightly older ones, there was the immensely popular "Sindy" doll, who was first introduced in 1951 and is still going strong today. Previously, most dolls had been like babies, but Sindy was very definitely a teenage doll: she had a range of outfits for different occasions and went out with a boy called Paul. (There was an equivalent American doll, Barbie, with a boyfriend called Ken.) A girl of the 1950s explains the appeal of Sindy:

The great thing about Sindy was that she was a fashion doll. There were all sorts of ways of experimenting with her appearance and clothes. Even quite young girls had a Sindy doll — before the 1950s, girls of ten had been just schoolchildren, but my generation were already beginning to experiment with make-up and were conscious of fashion.
(Penny Williams, b. 1949)

Other toys popular in the 1950s were the plastic animals which could be arranged on a model farm, the Meccano sets and other constructional toys. The many modern toys that are spin-offs from the television and other media were still largely in the future, although there was a great vogue for Noddy and Big Ears toys (from the books by Enid Blyton and later on television) and for Larry the Lamb toys (he was the star of radio's *Toytown*, and later transferred to television as a puppet). Board games were also popular with older children, although there was not today's wide choice: there was Monopoly and Ludo, but more modern games, such as Cluedo, had not yet been marketed.

One phenomenon that began in the 1950s was the "craze" — an amusement that suddenly becomes popular among teenagers and younger children everywhere for a brief period. Recent examples have been skateboarding, Rubik cubes and stereo-while-you-walk-around. In the mid-1950s, the first of these crazes was for the "hula-hoop". These hoops were spun by moving at the waist, in imitation of Hawaiian hula dancers, and they were popular especially among girls.

Comics

Comics were changing fast in the 1950s. The equivalent of "comics" before 1950 had really been boys' or girls' "papers". They did not usually have stories in pictures, but long written stories with some illustrations. The older papers for boys, such as *Rover*, *Champion* and *Hotspur*, specialized in the school story, as boys' papers had done for many years. For example in *Hotspur*, there were stories of the Red Circle School, a public school so-called because there were three houses, built of red sandstone and forming a circle around a central quadrangle, and containing boys from Britain, North America and all parts of the British Empire. The boys had names like "Spiv Ranger" and "Wild Cat McCoy", and there were teachers like Mr Alfred Smugg and the popular Dixie Dale. The stories had long, colourful titles such as "Caned Six Times in his First Day at School" and "Never Hang a Big Shot by his Braces". These stories were popular with all types of boys, even those not at public school. Frank Johnson, now a leading journalist and in the early 1950s at a secondary modern school in the East End, explained in the *Daily Telegraph* in 1977:

Rover and *Hotspur* were still favoured by us. And for Christmas an aunt who would never have set foot in a public school except as a cleaner would think it a matter of course to give her nephew *The Fifth Form at St Dominic's*, a morality involving the eventual downfall of Loman, a cad. None of us knew any Latin tags. The language was not taught. Nor, indeed, on the whole was English, so we were not strong on Shakespearian quotations either. But the phrase "Flashman! You are a bully and a liar and there is no place for you in this school" was understood among us as emanating from the incomparable "Tom Brown's Schooldays". It was used by us ironically.

49

47   Some 1950s annuals.

But boys' comics were changing. After the war, some comics came from America, called "horror comics", which featured gory stories of criminals and monsters and were feared by parents as being bad for children. In 1950, one of the most popular comics of the decade, *Eagle*, was launched as an answer to the "horror comics"; it would be modern, but also have high standards. *Eagle* was a mixture of stories in pictures and written stories with some illustrations, and had a wide variety of types of story, including Westerns, war stories and space stories. It also featured true stories, in comic-strip form, of historical heroes like Alfred the Great and St Vincent de Paul, as well as news of sport and boys' activities. The front page featured the adventures of the intrepid space pilot, Dan Dare, who became

a great children's hero of the 1950s. *Eagle* also had a version for younger boys, called *Robin*, while another similar paper (later merged with *Eagle*) was *Swift*.

There was a wide choice of comics and children's papers in the 1950s. *Dandy* and *Beano* were very popular, as they were before and have been since, while *Film Fun* and *Radio Fun* had their devoted circles of young readers. *Enid Blyton's Magazine* was popular among children who read her books, while a highly educational paper for younger readers was *The Young Elizabethan*. The main 1950s comic for girls was *Girl*, started in 1951, although it was hoped that this would appeal to both sexes. 1958 was the first year of *Bunty*, a more modern comic for girls, which has retained its great popularity ever since. The next year saw the launch of *Boyfriend*, the first of a new type of magazine aimed at teenage girls whose interest in the opposite sex was awakening.

Books

Reading was becoming more popular in the
1950s, with both children and adults, and
growing affluence was allowing more young
people to build up their own personal
collection of books. This trend was limited,
however, by the high cost of children's books
(between 1955 and 1960 the price rose on
average from 8s 6d to 12s 6d), which was
largely caused by the majority of children's
books still being in hardback only. Paper-
backs for adults had first become common
in the 1930s, and the children's imprint of
Penguin Books, Puffin, started in 1941. But
progress in publishing titles was slow and the
100th Puffin Book (*The Puffin Song Book*
by Leslie Woodgate) was not reached until
1956. It was not until the rapid development
of other paperback publishing houses for
children in the 1960s, that the child's
personal collection of books became really
common.

48   Quiet consultation at a junior library.

This meant that most children who read a
lot relied on children's public libraries, and
these were developing well during the decade.
There were also at this period lending
libraries run by the shop chains Boots and
W. H. Smith and many circulating libraries
that came round to people's houses in vans.
Britain had a tradition of children's public
library provision, dating back to the closing
years of the nineteenth century, but often
the "children's library" had been a mere
corner of a larger room, where there was no
specialist children's librarian, and children
sometimes had to choose books, without
seeing them, from a catalogue. But all this
was improving: the Youth Libraries Section
of the Library Association had been founded
in 1947, led by redoubtable ladies like
Eileen Colwell and Phyllis Parrott, and new
developments such as story hour in the

library, links with schools in the shape of class visits, and the broadening of library activities, were all encouraged.

But children's libraries had still not reached the modern stage of comfort, accessibility and bright, cheerful decor. Brian Brown, who started in children's librarianship in the 1950s and is now Schools Librarian in Sutton, Surrey, recalls what many children's libraries were like in the early days:

> There were wooden chairs at tables in the centre of the room with the books placed rather forbiddingly on dark-oak shelves at the sides of the room. The colourful dust-jackets were taken off the books for fear they would get spoilt, so they were in dull green, brown and red bindings. The silence notices and fines for late books were still very common, and there was a general atmosphere of formality and insistence on behaviour.

A very large number of excellent writers for children began working in the 1950s, so that the age has come to be spoken of as a "golden age of children's literature" — although the books that were enjoyed most by children were not always the ones which won the Carnegie Medal (the children's book award) or were most approved of by librarians. A survey of children's reading habits, carried out in 1957, showed that the most popular author for boys was Captain W. E. Johns, whose stories about the airman *Biggles* had long been favourites, while the most popular author overall was Enid Blyton, whose books had first become immensely widely read in the war years and who wrote long-running series like *The Secret Seven*, *The Famous Five* and *Noddy and Big Ears*. By the late 1950s some children's libraries had decided not to stock Enid Blyton books, on the grounds that her style was over-simple and did not foster reading development, although the evidence was that she had a unique gift

for appealing to and understanding children's imaginations.

At a rather higher literary level, there were many excellent authors whose books were extremely popular. Picture books for children were at a peak, with the excellent works of Edward Ardizzone, who created the character of Little Tim, and Kathleen Hale, who wrote and illustrated the stories of the cat *Orlando*. Historical fiction for young readers (more popular in the 1950s than it is now, perhaps because formal history was more often taught in schools) had many excellent practitioners, such as Cynthia Harnett, Geoffrey Trease and Henry Treece. The school story was still popular, with authors such as Anthony Buckeridge who wrote the *Jennings* stories, while the "career" stories of Noel Streatfield were also widely read. A large number of authors wrote stories about everyday life (authors like E. W. Hildick, John Rowe Townsend and Geoffrey Trease), while science fiction and fantasy were perhaps less popular than now (the space age was just starting). But science fiction had excellent practitioners like Donald Suddaby, while C. S. Lewis's *Narnia* books opened up a rich world of fantasy for children. There was also a growing choice of non-fiction for children, although not as wide as today.

At a higher level even than these excellent books were several outstanding masterpieces for children. *Tom's Midnight Garden* by Philippa Pearce was published in 1955, a rich and beautiful novel which brings it own special twist to the familiar "timeswitch" theme. During the decade, Rosemary Sutcliff was developing as a brilliant author of demanding but highly rewarding historical novels, and she reached her height in *The Lantern Bearers* (1959). This is the story of a young Roman officer who decides that duty lies in staying in Britain when the Roman legions leave. It is a moving master-piece which can be enjoyed by adults as much as by young readers. Another out-

standing book in 1959 was *The Fair to Middling* by Arthur Calder Marshall, the story of a group of handicapped orphans who visit a magic fair where they get the chance to see what would happen if their dreams of health and happiness came true. The book might perhaps be found strange and depressing by some children, but provides a real expansion of the imagination for those capable of responding to its humour, wisdom and sadness.

The Cinema

The cinema had been the great treat of the week for thirty years in Britain before the 1950s, but now it began to suffer the fatal competition of television and audience figures fell inexorably. However, for most of the decade, the "Saturday morning flicks" was a great feature of the week for many children, when they could see special children's programmes of cowboy films, space adventures and cartoons.

The cinema continued to provide delights for children in the 1950s. The film companies had to think of gimmicks to try to counter the decline in audience figures, and so children could experience the interest of the various "wide screen" systems, such as Cinerama, and the first experiments in 3D-vision, which came in 1952, and which were

53

advertised with the alarming but thrilling promise that you could have "a lion in your lap". There were also many colourful films appealing to children, such as the Walt Disney cartoons, of which *Peter Pan* was a 1950s example. Perhaps the most successful Disney film of all, *The Adventures of Davy Crockett*, was released in 1955, and soon had the nation's children all going round in the Western hero's distinguishing raccoon skin headgear. A boy of the 1950s recalls:

> I very much remember the sensation caused by the film of *Davy Crockett*. All the kids round our way were mad on it, and all of them were wearing that headgear — you know, those fur hats with "tails" hanging down from the back of them.
> (Peter Willis, b. 1944)

50   Child's play.

Television and Radio

One of the very greatest changes in the 1950s for the average family would have been the coming of the television. At the beginning of the 1950s, radio was still the great national entertainment and information medium, and a mere 350,000 households, grouped in large cities, had a television set. The hours of broadcasting on television were restricted; there were only BBC services (as with radio); and in the *Radio Times* the columns listing television programmes were tucked away on an inconspicuous page at the back. Televisions were tiny by modern standards (a nine- or ten-inch screen was standard), and television sets had a pair of double doors which were always kept closed when the set was not on, as if people feared that the unpredictable box might be watching *them*.

During the 1950s all this started to change. By 1952 there were two million sets in use, and many more families bought their first set so that they could watch the coronation in 1953. But the real breakthrough came after the introduction of the independent broadcasting stations in 1955, which provided a more popular and up-to-date type of programme than the BBC had traditionally done. There was an immense rush to buy sets, and by the end of the decade the great majority of homes had one. The television was on in the average home for five hours a day in winter and three-and-a-half in summer. All sets were still black-and-white, however; colour television was not introduced until the later 1960s.

The introduction of the television caused great controversy. In the 1950s there were many families who boasted that they did not possess the new-fangled invention and parents who denied their children's pleas for one. There was a widespread belief that watching TV could give people various diseases, ruin their eyesight and posture, and give children what was known as "TV neck". It was feared that the television would expose children to violence and crime on the screen (fears that have not died today). A girl growing up in the 1950s reflects on the change:

I think the television must have been the biggest change in the lives of children this century. Before that, they must have spent so much more of their time out, exploring, especially in summer. I remember how it changed our lives — it gave us a wonderful sense of entertainment, but I also think it meant we discovered less for ourselves than previous generations of children did.
(Penny Williams, b. 1949)

This is one view of television. It could also be argued that television brought families

51 and 52   First presenters of *Blue Peter*: Christopher Trace and Leila Williams.

together and gave them a common focus of interest. An East End woman at the time said:

> It didn't destroy conversation for us. It *was* the conversation. I don't know what we talked about before.

As the decade went on, television became more and more all-pervasive. Before 1957, the time between six and seven in the evening was known as the "toddlers' truce", an hour when the television was off and parents could get children off to bed. But this was discontinued when BBC's popular current affairs programme, *Tonight*, started.

The spread of television meant that the radio audience declined immensely. The average regular audience fell from around nine million in 1954 to three-and-a-half million in 1957. The generation of the early 1950s was the last to enjoy BBC's traditional *Children's Hour* on radio, with its entertaining but instructive tone, its stories, snippets of classical music and its tea parties. The radio programme for very small children, *Listen with Mother*, remained popular throughout the 1950s (and almost until the present day) with its catchline, when the story started, "Are you sitting comfortably? Then I'll begin." Other radio programmes for adults, such as *The Navy Lark* and *The Goon Show*, were very popular with the young, as was *The Adventures of Dick Barton, Special Agent* at the beginning of the decade (the BBC killed him off in 1951).

Television brought a wider range of programmes to children. The television equivalent of *Listen with Mother* was *Watch with Mother*, and on the five different days of the week (in 1959) a child could watch *Picture Book*, *Andy Pandy*, *The Flowerpot Men*, *Rag, Tag and Bobtail* and *The Woodentops*. Enid Blyton told stories about Noddy on *Small Time* on BBC, while on ITV the adventures of Rin-Tin-Tin, the famous alsatian, were very popular. One immensely successful BBC programme which began in 1958 and is still going strong is *Blue Peter*. Leila Williams and Christopher Trace were the first of a long series of charming, enterprising and much-loved presenters which the programme has had. In the late 1950s there were many excellent historical series for children: one favourite was *The Adventures of Robin Hood* — which had Britain's children dressing in Lincoln Green and playing with bows and arrows. Also by the end of the decade, the American cartoon series, such as *Popeye* and *The Adventures of Huckleberry Hound* had started to be shown, while if they stayed up after supper, children could watch more historical adventure stories like *Ivanhoe*, thrilling Westerns like *Rawhide*, the new type of prize-money quiz-shows like *Take your Pick* (with its conflicting cries of "take the money!" or "open the box!"), or human-interest drama series such as the hospital series *Emergency Ward Ten*.

Sport

The 1950s had created a more fit and vigorous type of young person, owing to the improvements in health care, and this, together with growing affluence, helped to encourage participation in sport. New sports and techniques became available; for example, the cheap outboard motor and build-it-yourself kits encouraged boating. It was estimated that two million people, including many of the young, regularly went fishing. Three times as many people as before the war were learning to ride horses. Sporting heroes like the runner Roger Bannister and the cricketer Don Bradman were very popular.

But the most popular British sport, especially for the young male, remained football. True, the coming of television meant that some of the old Saturday ritual of fathers and sons going to "the match" tended to vanish, but three-quarters of a million men and youths played football seriously for their own enjoyment in the early 1950s, and there were nearly 3,000 amateur teams playing in local Sunday leagues. Then as now, the great teams had their dedicated clubs of supporters, although the problems of vandalism and hooliganism sadly associated with this had not reached their modern proportions. On a national level, football gained an extra interest from Britain's participation in the World Cup from 1950, although for many years British teams did not do very well.

Holidays

The new world of affluence changed the British holiday too. Gone were the traditional working-class holiday patterns of "wakes week" in the north and hop-picking in Kent for Londoners. In contrast, the 1950s saw the real beginning of the foreign holiday

53 The new car.

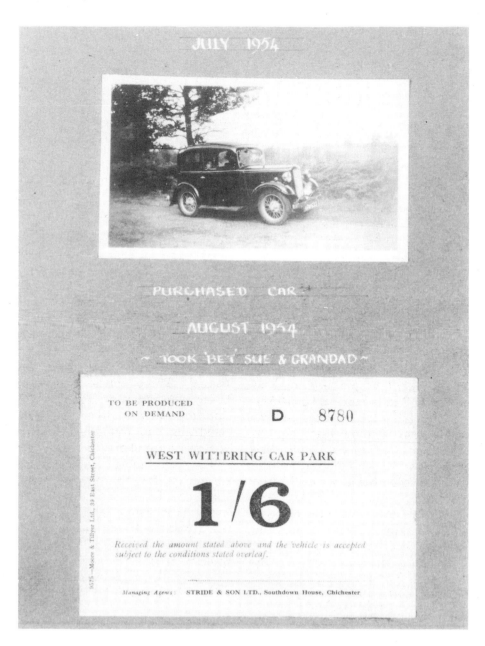

JULY 1954

PURCHASED CAR

AUGUST 1954

~ TOOK BET SUE & GRANDAD ~

TO BE PRODUCED ON DEMAND   D   8780

WEST WITTERING CAR PARK

1/6

Received the amount stated above and the vehicle is accepted subject to the conditions stated overleaf.

Managing Agents: STRIDE & SON LTD., Southdown House, Chichester

9575—Moore & Tillyer Ltd., 39 East Street, Chichester

for everyone. In 1952, the airlines introduced the first "tourist" fares, and by 1958 the number of Britons going on foreign holidays had reached two million, twice the pre-war figure, although still small by modern standards. Not only was Britain itself becoming more cosmopolitan, but the British now also got the chance to sample "abroad" for themselves. Teenagers of the 1950s inaugurated the modern practice of travelling around the continent hitching lifts, or by scooter or cycle.

The spread of the family motor car (there was one car to every seven families at the beginning of the decade and one car to every three-and-a-half at the end of it) meant that people could explore their own country for themselves in a way they had previously never been able to, and so city children from a young age knew the narrow coves of Cornwall, the upland "dales" of Yorkshire or the magnificent lakes and fells of Cumbria. But the organized holiday was just as popular: the 1950s were the great years of the "holiday camp", and millions went to the centres run by Butlins and Pontins, often at the seaside, where they stayed in holiday chalets and enjoyed swimming pools, playgrounds, sports and, for the adults, cabarets laid on at night.

Organized Activities for the Young

The 1950s also saw a great expansion in organized activities to help the young enjoy their leisure and develop their personalities. This began in the schools, with a new world of school visits, activities and clubs. How important this was in breaking down the isolation from which some children had suffered is illustrated by the story of the educator Richard West who, when a teacher at Walworth School in south London in the late 1950s, took the children on a visit to the South Kensington museums and found it was the first time that many of them had been north of the river Thames.

Outside school, there was now a proliferation of youth centres and youth clubs, provided by the local authorities who had been encouraged by the Government to institute them after the war. A fully-qualified Youth Service Officer network had been developed to work in these clubs. At the beginning of the decade, it was estimated that, over Britain as a whole, four in every ten people between the ages of fourteen and eighteen belonged to some sort of club. By the end of the decade, it began to be thought normal for the young to be members of clubs, and much worried discussion surrounded the problem of "unclubbables". At the same time, many of the young preferred to make their own amusements in the new coffee bars and jazz clubs which were springing up.

Alongside all this new activity, the traditional organizations for the young, such as the Scouts and Guides (with their younger equivalents of Wolf Cubs and Brownies), the Boys' Brigade and the boys' clubs, continued to be very popular, perhaps slightly more so than now. The scout movement (scouts and cubs) had 471,364 members in 1950, which had risen to 571,402 members by 1959, although the movement was increasingly

◄ 54 Campers outside their chalet at Butlin's, Filey, Yorkshire.

stronger with the younger age groups than with the older. Great events in 1950s scouting history were the seventh world Jamboree, held in Austria in 1951 and attracting scouts from many nations, and an extra jamboree held in 1957 for the movement's 50th anniversary. "Bob-a-Job-week" had been introduced in 1949 and soon proved popular. During the decade, the scout movement continued to teach its traditional ideals of service, discipline and preparedness, but the emphasis on empire-building was gradually dropped, and the movement kept up with the times by forsaking the big broad-brimmed hats in favour of berets and by holding reviews on uniform.

Interest in Science

A new component of 1950s leisure was the growing interest of the young in science. As we have said, science study was becoming increasingly popular in the schools, and interest was encouraged by the fact that the 1950s were years of great scientific advances

and achievements. The decade saw the dawning of the "space age": it was in 1957 that the Russians launched the first satellite or "sputnik"; in the second sputnik they sent up the dog Laika; and in 1959 they photographed the far side of the moon. Other advances were the first jet airliners, the opening of the Jodrell Bank radio telescope in 1957, and the opening of Calder Hall in Cumbria, the world's first large-scale nuclear power station, in 1956. At the level of the home, the 1950s was the dawning of the age of modern electronics, with a new entertainment world opened up by hi-fi, and the age of the transistor beginning at the end of the decade.

The interest in science's achievements expressed itself in many ways. One of the most well-supported events of the 1950s was the annual "Boys' and Girls' Exhibition" held at Olympia in London, which concentrated on science, and whose theme in 1956 was the new world of space travel. At a more popular level, it was in the early 1950s that the first sightings were made of unidentified flying objects (UFOs), which soon gained the nickname of "flying saucers".

55 Youth club members, 1957.

6 The Birth of the Teenager

At the beginning of the 1950s the word "teenager" would not have been understood by most people. For many centuries before modern times people thought simply in terms of childhood and adulthood — with even children being thought of largely as miniature or training adults. At a certain stage (leaving school at 14 in early twentieth-century England, or at the time of initiation ceremonies in primitive societies), the child achieved adulthood and was immediately expected to drop all the habits and expectations of childhood. During the greater part of human history, the teenager — the adolescent — did not exist.

The modern teenager really dates from the 1950s. Some idea of there being a period of adolescence does date back to the late eighteenth century, but it was only applied to the children of the well-off, and there was no real idea that adolescents might want to have fashions, music and a lifestyle of their own. At the beginning of the 1950s the phrase "pop music" was also not widely understood and the popular music of the time, such as the "swing" bands and the "crooners", was really aimed at an adult age group. During the 1950s all this changed, and the main reason was that the affluent society had given a new spending power to the young, who might not have left school and were often earning good money if they had. By the early 1950s the earnings of teenagers had increased by 50 per cent in value since 1938 and their spending capacity by 100 per cent, taking inflation into account. The significance of the change was noted at the time by an acute observer of 1950s youth, Colin MacInnes, in his book *England, Half English*:

> Today, youth has money, and teenagers have become a power. In their struggle to impose their wills upon the adult world, young men and women have always been blessed with energy, but never, until now, with wealth. After handing a pound or two over to Mum, they are left with more spending money than most of their elders, crushed by adult obligations. They are a social group whose tastes are studied with respect — particularly by the entertainment industry.

The New Music

Their new power and wealth gave the teenagers the freedom to create their own life and to rebel against their elders, choosing their own heroes like the early-dying, eternally-misunderstood James Dean and the dangerous Marlon Brando, roaring round in black leather on his motorbike: both these were American film-stars. It was America, too, that produced the new music that was to seem to youth to be its own characteristic expression — rock'n roll. It was in 1955 that Bill Haley and his Comets developed a new sound with the film *Rock Around the Clock*, which, when it was shown in Britain in 1956, had teenagers rising from their seats in the audiences to bounce and jive in the aisles as they had never done before, and which caused riots in London's Elephant and Castle when

2,000 young people were reported to have taken to the streets in an orgy of violence and vandalism.

Haley visited Britain in 1957, but he was over thirty and not a romantic figure. Soon, younger heroes were rising to exploit the crude, vigorous, youthful music he had created. The greatest phenomenon among these was the American truck-driver from Memphis, Elvis Presley, who sang in the mid-1950s songs like "Hound Dog", "All Shook Up", "Jailhouse Rock" and "Hard-Hearted Woman". No British singer or group was to gain equal fame until the Beatles arrived in the 1960s, but there were soon British singers who sang pop music similar to that of the rock n' roll singers: Cliff Richard, and the boy from Bermondsey who became a star, Tommy Steele, who spoke with a Cockney accent and sang in a transatlantic whine. Colin MacInnes explains his appeal:

> The most striking feature of Tommy's performance is that it is both animally sensual and innocent, pure. He is Pan, he is Puck, he is every nice young girl's boy, every kid's favourite elder brother, every mother's cherished adolescent son. His charmingly ugly, melancholy, cheeky countenance and his elfin body with its gesticulations like an electric eel, are irresistibly engaging. . .

Soon, there were legions of young pop singers, all singing a new rhythmical, raw music appealing to the teenage market: singers like Marty Wilde, Billy Fury, Adam Faith, Johnny Gentle, Vince Eager, all of them usually with middle-aged backing groups interjecting noises like "waah", "bup bup" or "sh-boom boom". The songs they sang would seem simple by modern standards, with little variation and words like:

> I love you with all my heart
> And I hope we will never part.

56   Bill Haley on his tour of Britain, 1957.

This was largely a teenage music, but it soon became the typical music of the age, appealing to and impressing even quite young children. A child of the 1950s speaks of the impression made by *Living Doll*, Cliff Richard's hit, which was in the charts in 1959:

> One of my earliest memories is the impression made on me by *Living Doll*. I can't have been more than about six or seven at the time. It really is one of the things I remember clearest.
> (Rupert Wood, b. 1952)

Soon, the new music was being allowed onto the normally staid and respectable BBC,

Elvis in *Jail House Rock.*

with programmes like *Six-Five Special* and *Juke Box Jury* where a panel of people voted new records either a "Hit" or a "Miss". Older types of music — the ballad songs of the "crooners" for instance — were still popular, especially among older people, but the age when "rock" is the dominant sound of modern popular music can be said to have begun in the 1950s.

Teenage Styles, Tastes and Gangs
The new pop music was the most characteristic and noticeable expression of the 1950s teenager, but it was by no means the only one. The first sign of adolescent fashion had appeared at the end of the 1940s with the "spiv" suits and the craze for jiving and jazz-clubs. Jazz, especially of the "modernist" variety, remained immensely popular during the 1950s, although appealing increasingly to a slightly older and more sophisticated audience than the teenagers.

In 1953 and 1954 the first of the teenage "gangs" or "sub-cultures" appeared. These were the "teddy boys" or "teds", and their distinctive style spread from working-class south London, which was their heartland, to all parts of the country. Their dress was a sort of parody of the upper-class fashions of fifty years before, the Edwardian age: they had drainpipe trousers, long jackets with velvet cuffs and collars, and wore hair that was long for that period and slicked down with Brylcreem. They became much feared by adults at the time, sometimes with good reason, as they pursued gang warfare and vandalism in the streets and dance halls. In 1953, a group of teds was involved in the murder of a youth on Clapham Common in south London, and in 1958, teddy boys were among the foremost provokers of the Notting Hill riots, in which white people protested violently about coloured immigrants coming to Britain. Similar groups to the teddy boys appeared in all parts of Europe at the same time, and they were to be the first of a long line of teenage groups: mods and rockers, skinheads and hippies, punk rockers.

As the decade continued, more peaceful youth styles emerged. Jazz clubs continued to be popular. Dance-halls and ice-rinks provided other popular teenage entertainments and a chance to get to know the opposite sex. The young now rode around on motor scooters or motorbikes (the car of one's own, already common in America, was

58 Tommy Steele (centre right) and his rock 'n roll band.

still usually a dream in Britain) and they patronized the coffee bars that were springing up on the high streets, serving "espresso coffee" and offering a juke-box. The record shops now abounded with self-service "browseries" and "melody bars", where the young could buy what was defined as the latest sound. In the late 1950s the wearing of "Italian-style" clothes had become fashionable — very short hanging surcoat and skin-tight leg-wear for the boys; for the girls, mascara, cotton blouses, paper-nylon petticoats and stiletto heels. Chains of special shops arose, to sell the new teenage fashions, which also now included jeans, jumpers (new at the time) and "sack" dresses.

The young entered a whole new world of excitement. Sir John Wolfenden, Vice-Chancellor of Reading University, noted "a kind of emotional, hectic flush about many young people today". Their parents were often worried by this: the teenage culture was new, and 1950s youngsters had to cope

59   Teddy boys at a dance hall, Tottenham, London, 1954.

60   Factory workers at a youth club, 1958.

more often than teenagers today with parental arguments about dress, length of hair, boyfriends, visits to dance halls and late nights. The youth culture of the 1950s, though powerful, only really affected a minority of young people. It was only with the more thoroughgoing youth revolt of the 1960s that the freedom of the young to manage their own lives was substantially accepted.

Youth Problems: Delinquency, Crime, Sex

The youth culture had its positive side, but the revolt of youth could have consequences harmful to society and provoked worries about a loss of discipline. These fears were by no means unfounded: crimes by offenders under twenty-one in England rose from 24,000 in 1955 to 45,000 in 1959. Vandalism and violence were on the increase — the inevitable but unwanted concomitant of the increase in youth's freedom and assertiveness.

There were new measures in the 1950s to cope with juvenile crime and offenders. The legal procedure had been revised in 1948, with new methods short of custodial sentences being introduced, such as periods of probation and requiring young offenders to report regularly to attendance centres. Custodial solutions were resorted to more often than in the 1970s and 1980s, however, although many of the approved schools and borstals of the time were in old, unsuitable and forbidding buildings, where discipline was often harsh.

Sex among teenagers was also causing increasing concern in the 1950s. The modern trend towards more personal and moral freedom, as well as the tendency to grow up faster, meant that the problem was more evident — but the 1950s were only at the start of the trend towards "permissiveness". Teenagers were usually told that "necking" might be just permissible, but anything further, like "heavy petting", was severely discouraged. Young people growing up homosexual still had very little provision

61   Menial work for borstal boys.

made for their needs: they were often left to gain what enlightenment they could from the few novels that had been published, which dealt with the subject, such as *The Charioteer* by Mary Renault (1953), and they had to cope with the fact that the expression of their emotions (if they were male) would be against the law when they were adults.

The lack of freedom in sexual matters was very galling for the young, but some real problems were on the increase: there had never, for instance, been so many unmarried mothers and they had never

65

62 Apprentices at the Derby Locomotive Works School.

college was becoming less abrupt in the 1950s. In the schools, a new careers service had been set up to prepare the young for the world of work, and visits to factories and other places of work were common for secondary modern school pupils. Once the young people got to work, there were more often than before some formal training schemes, and so the atmosphere of education did not entirely vanish. Also, more young people than ever before were taking spare-time jobs while still at school and gaining experience of work that way. This was not, of course, entirely new: the career of the English newspaper boy, for instance, can be traced back to the reign of Queen Anne (1702-1714) and much child-labour had been used in the nineteenth century. Legislation now prevented the exploitation of the young at work. But what was new was the trend for young people from all classes to take weekend and spare-time jobs, usually quite menial, but adding to their spending power and enabling them to enjoy teenage amusements. The catering group, J. Lyons and Co, inserted in the personal columns of *The Times* this tribute to their schoolboy helpers:

> Many of the lads are prefects, enjoying during term the dignity attaching to their seniority: yet with no sense of "side" — too often a weakness of previous generations — they have scrubbed floors, poured tea, washed up, with a shoulder-to-the-wheel enthusiasm which, in the opinion of Lyons, augurs well for the future of Britain.

More and more, appropriate training and qualifications were necessary for jobs (as one wit remarked, boys no longer "ran away to sea", they took a course for cabin boys Grade II). In 1947 there had been only 167,000 young workers receiving part-time education; by 1952 the number had expanded to 300,000, with 80 types of jobs or pro-

been so young (in Manchester, for example, the numbers of unmarried mothers under 15 doubled between 1954 and 1959). On the other hand, some of the other problems that have since become associated with youth were still uncommon in the 1950s. Surveys of the period actually reported a decrease in the problem of juvenile drunkenness: the coffee-bars sold just coffee, while Coca-Cola was still considered a daring teenage drink. Nor was drug-taking at all common among the young, in the 1950s, although it was to spread so rapidly in the 1960s and 1970s.

Work and College

The transition from school to work or to

fessions participating in the schemes. There was increasing interest in "sandwich courses", although the institution of day release was still quite rare.

The most common form of training for young workers was apprenticeship, which absorbed no less than one-third of all school leavers in 1959 (the comparable figure was 14 per cent in 1980). This was a five- or seven-year training for a skilled craftsman's job, and though it was more common in the 1950s than it is now, it might have been worth less — there was no national regulation of apprenticeship schemes, so the value of the training depended on the firm where it was done; apprentices were sometimes viewed as "cheap labour" and firms would take on more apprentices than they needed, not offering jobs to some when the course ended. There was also a high drop-out rate, because the training course could be hard, as an apprentice of the 1950s, John Stroud, now an engineering training officer, explains:

In the 1950s day-release to study at technical colleges was unknown. Apprentices were expected to attend night-classes at evening institutes, and had to attend three or four nights a week for up to five years — naturally, the drop-out rate was high. Only the really persistent and ambitious tended to stay the course.

One feature of apprenticeship in the 1950s was that it was virtually confined to boys. During this era, women were still not really encouraged to have careers, and provisions for training them were not good. Most girls still expected to work only for a few years before getting married, and this was true even of highly-educated girls: in 1959, an article in *The Guardian* reported that a group of Cambridge girl undergraduates had agreed that politics was not a good career for a woman because it could not be reconciled with marriage, and after marriage only

63　New arrivals at the Royal Fusiliers Barracks in Dover, 1956.

an exceptional woman would work outside her home. These attitudes were gradually changing, but the real stirring of women's liberation did not begin until the 1960s.

Going to some form of college after leaving school was becoming increasingly possible and popular during the 1950s. University education had previously been possible only for children of the well-off, but the proportion of young people going to university in the early 1950s was one-in-thirty rather than one-in-sixty as before the war. University places multiplied sevenfold during the decade, and new universities were designated at Nottingham, Southampton and Birmingham, although the really large expansion had to wait for the 1960s.

Other types of college were expanding too. At the beginning of the decade, it was generally agreed that provision for technical colleges was inadequate (one government inspector found a technical college established in a railway station and premises, and one class being held in a waiting room). However, there was a great increase in funding later in the decade; new colleges were built, and there was the introduction

67

'Well, gentlemen, I think we all fought a good fight . . .'

64   Retrospect.

of a graduate-equivalent qualification, the Diploma in Technology. Also becoming much more common in the 1950s were art colleges, business colleges and commerce schools — although the polytechnics were not introduced until the 1960s.

One feature of the transition to adulthood for young males in the 1950s was national service. This was retained in the 1950s, even though the war was over, because the international situation was still tense and Britain had more international commitments than it has now. There was usually two years' full-time service and the age of call-up was 18, although it was possible to gain deferment if you were following an apprenticeship or a university course, while people in certain reserved occupations (such as clergy or those in government posts abroad) did not have

to serve. There were mixed feelings at the time about national service. People who had originally been reluctant to serve sometimes came to have a nostalgic affection for the regimental-sergeant-major and the NAAFI canteen, while there were others who felt that military service encouraged discipline and halted the growth of crime and vandalism. But there were some who blamed military service for delinquency, and it was often resented because it was an interruption to adult life: youths who knew they would be called up at 18 often did little in the meantime but drift around from job to job and listen to rock n' roll. By the end of the 1950s it was decided to phase out national service; the last intake was in early 1961 and these served until 1963.

Retrospect

As they moved on to their adult lives in the 1960s, the young of the 1950s increasingly found that the promises of their childhood were fulfilled. The factories and offices where they went to work were bright, airy and safe and the hours were congenial; at the end of the 1950s the 42-hour week was still being worked, but the five-day week had become usual. Outside work, there was a new world of leisure and ease, and the activities, options and goods available to them had come to seem limitless. The 1950s had opened with shortages, and the choice had not been quite so wide then, but their adult world of freedom and opportunity was certainly one for which their childhood and youth in the 1950s had prepared them.

Date List

1950   (February) Labour Party returned to power with much-reduced majority.
1951   (May) Festival of Britain.
              (October) Conservative Party returned to power.
1952   (February) Death of George VI.
              (March) Identity cards abolished in Britain.
1953   (June) Coronation of Queen Elizabeth II.
              (June) Everest conquered.
1954   (July) Food rationing ends in Britain.
1955   Film of *Rock around the Clock*.
1956   (October) Hungarian uprising.
              (October) Suez crisis begins.
1957   (March) Ghana becomes independent.
              (October) Russians launch first Sputniks.
1958   (January) The Common Market comes into force.
1959   (October) Conservatives increase their majority for the third time.
              First section of M1 motorway opened in Britain.

Books for Further Reading

Harris, Nathaniel, *The Forties and Fifties, an illustrated history*, Macdonald Educational, 1975
Hopkins, Harry, *The New Look*, Secker & Warburg, 1963
Lewis, Peter, *The Fifties*, Heinemann, 1978
Pascall, Jeremy, *Growing up in the Fifties*, Wayland, 1980

Acknowledgments

The author would like to thank the following who shared with him their experience of growing up in the 1950s: Brian Brown, Rhys Burriss, Bob Crabtree, Zara Sandler, John Stroud, Penny Williams, Peter Willis, Rupert Wood.

The author, on holiday in Brussells.

Bob Crabtee and his older brother.

Zara Sandler with her baby daughter Jacqui.

70

Index

The numbers in **bold type** refer to the figure numbers of the illustrations

Adventures of Davy Crockett, The 54; **49**
affluent society 5
all-age schools 29
Anne, Princess 10
apprenticeship 67
architecture 14, 38ff; **12**
Attlee, Clement 6
austerity, age of 6

baby boom 15
Bannister, Roger 10, 56
Bevin, Ernest 13
birth 14
Blue Peter 56; **51, 52**
Blyton, Enid 49, 52
bombsites 43
books 51ff
borstals 65
Bowlby, Dr John 18f
Boys' and Girls' Exhibition 59
Bradman, Don 56
Britain
  economic problems of 13
  world position of 10ff
budgie boom 21
Bunty 50

Calder-Marshall, Arthur, *The Fair to Middling* 52
Charles, Prince 10
child care 18ff
children's homes 23f
Children's Hour 23f
Church of England 21
Churchill, Winston 6
cinemas 53f
Clean Air Act 43
clothes 16, 64
comics 49f
comprehensive schools 34f
Conservative Party 6, 35
corner shops 45

Coronation of Elizabeth II 9, 13
crime 65

Dinky Toys 48; **45**
Diploma in Technology 68
direct grant schools 33
discipline, home 18f, 64f

Eagle 50
East End of London 19, 40f
Eden, Anthony 6, 12
education 25ff
Education Act of 1944 25, 27, 29
eleven plus 29
Elizabeth II 6, 9; **3, 6**
Elizabeth, the Queen Mother 6; **3**
Eton 36
European Economic Community (EEC) 12
Everest, conquest of 10

family life 15f, 18ff
Festival of Britain 6ff
fire engines 6
food 20f
football 56f
furniture 21; **20, 21**

General Certificate of Education (GCE) 31
George VI 6; **3**
grammar schools 32ff

Haley, Bill 60f; **56**
health clinics 14f, 16
health schools 24
high-rise flats 40f
Hillary, Sir Edmund 10
hire purchase 13
holidays 57f
holiday camps 58
homosexuality 65

Hotspur 49
housing estates 40
hula-hoop 49; **16**
Hungarian Uprising 12
huts 27

immigrants 37
India 11

Janet and John Books 28
jazz 63
Johns, Captain W.E. 52
Johnson, Frank 49
Juke Box Jury 63

Kidbrooke Comprehensive School 25; **31**
King, Truby 18
Korean War 10

Labour Party 6, 35
latchkey kids 19
liberty bodice 17
libraries 51f
Listen with Mother 56
Living Doll 61

MacInnes, Colin 60, 61
Macmillan, Harold 6, 13; **4, 64**
Malaya 12; **9**
matchbox toys 48
Morrison, Herbert 8
motor car 39, 42f, 58; **53**
music 34

National Service 68; **63**
National Youth Orchestra 34
Nasser, Abdul Gamal 11
natural childbirth 14
New Elizabethan 10
new towns 35f
Notting Hill riots 63

overspill 38ff

Pearce, Philippa, *Tom's Midnight Garden* 52
pets 21
Piaget, Jean 19f, 29
politics 13
pre-fabs 41
Premium Bonds 13
Presley, Elvis 61; **57**
primary schools 27ff
Princess prams 16
privacy 21f
public schools 35f

radio 54ff
rationing 6, 20
record industry 64
Red Circle School 49
religion 20
Renault, Mary, *The Charioteer* 65
Richard, Cliff 61
Rock Around the Clock 60f
Roman Catholic Church 21, 37
Rover 49
Royal Festival Hall 8

science, interest in 58
Scouts, Cubs, Guides and Brownies 58f
secondary schools 29ff
secondary modern schools 30ff
Second World War 5, 10
sex 65
sherpa Sen Tenzing 10
short-back-and-sides 17
Sindy 48f
smog 6, 43; **1**
Soviet Union 10ff
Spock, Benjamin, Dr 18, 28
sport 56f
Steele, Tommy 61; **58**
Suez Crisis 11f
supermarkets 45f
Sutcliff, Rosemary, *The Lantern Bearers* 52
sweets 13, 20

Taylor, A.J.P. 30
teacher training 27
technical colleges 67
technical schools 34
teddy boys 63; **59**
teenagers 60ff

television 54ff
training 66f
trains 43
trams 43; **2**
tripartite system 25
trolleybuses 43

United States of America 10f, 60, 63
universities 67

vaccinations 15

Watch with Mother 56
Waugh, Evelyn 43
West, Richard 58
Willmott, Peter, *Adolescent Boys of East London* 32ff
Wolfenden, Sir John 64
women, position of 15, 19, 67
work 66ff

Young and Willmott, *Family and Kinship in East London* 40
Young Elizabethan 10, 50
Youth and Music 34
youth clubs 58; **55**